To order additional copies of
Illuminating Shadow Figures in Scripture,
by Chantal J. Klingbeil and Gerald A. Klingbeil, call **1-800-765-6955**.

Visit us at
www.reviewandherald.com
for information on other Review and Herald® products.

Illuminating SHADOW FIGURES in Scripture

Chantal J. Klingbeil & Gerald A. Klingbeil

REVIEW AND HERALD® PUBLISHING ASSOCIATION

Since 1861 | www.reviewandherald.com

Published by Review and Herald® Publishing Association, Hagerstown, MD 21741-1119

This book was
Edited by Kalie Kelch
Copyedited by James Hoffer
Designed by Ron J. Pride
Cover illustration by Joãu Luiz Cardozo
Interior designed by Heather Rogers
Typeset: Bembo 11/13

PRINTED IN U.S.A.

14 13 12 11 10   5 4 3 2 1

Library of Congress Cataloging-in-Publication Data
Klingbeil, Chantal J., 1970-   .
   Illuminating shadow figures in Scripture / Chantal J. Klingbeil and Gerald A. Klingbeil.
      p. cm.
   1. Bible. O.T.—Biography. I. Klingbeil, Gerald A., 1964- II. Title.
   BS571.K55 2010
   221.9'22—dc22

                              2009047609
ISBN 978-0-8280-2509-6

Dedicated to

Hannah, Sarah, and Jemima—
three precious blossoms that
unfold every day more of
God's wonderful grace.

Contents

Preface

This is a book about small people. No, we don't mean *short* people, but rather people we are often tempted to overlook when we read Scripture.

These people came from different places in life. Some got lucky and were born into leading, well-to-do families. Others were hard-working farmers or servants. Most of them came from Israel—but there were a number who did not enjoy the benefits of a Christian (Israelite) upbringing. Male and female, they all share one particular characteristic: their contribution and role in Scripture is often underrated.

We are intrigued by these people, and the mere fact that you purchased this book suggests that you are too. These were people who would not necessarily stand out in a crowd. By positive, but also negative, example, they tell us an important truth: notwithstanding your position in life, your gender, your heritage, your socio-economic situation, God is interested in working *in* you and *with* you.

In our first chapter we focus on the important concepts of *story* and *history* and introduce the particular characteristics of this volume, noting that each chapter follows the same outline. Each person is introduced in a unique and creative way (it was quite a challenge to avoid repetition here) and through categories—cast members, historical background, action, digging deep, and issues—we examine the lives of 12 Bible characters who are often overlooked. We end each chapter on a personal note, individually writing about a particular nuance of the story that spoke to us personally.

As you read this book, we hope you will become better acquainted with these shadow figures (as we did when we wrote the *Adult Sabbath School Bible Study Guide* as well as this volume). We also hope you will recognize that importance is not based on a place in the spotlight, but rather on the willingness to be used by a mighty God who loves all people.

—Chantal and Gerald Klingbeil

Chapter 1

From Story to History

Shadow Figures and the Lure of Stories

Shadow figures are difficult to pin down, especially when they appear in texts that are often hard to understand, come from a different era, have a distinct cultural background, and sound strange to us.

Shadow figures, however, are also very close to our hearts. We can identify with them. They seem to be closer to us and our sense of being, especially when we do not live in the White House or Buckingham Palace and when our names are not found in the tabloids or on pages 1 to 3 of the Washington *Post* or the *Frankfurter Allgemeine Zeitung*.

Every time somebody begins to tell a story in our family our three girls become very attentive and quiet as mice. They hang on every word and are anxious to soak in every detail of the story. Sometimes, playing the devil's advocate, we randomly interrupt the story and move to another unrelated topic. You can be sure that our daughters do not stand for it. They want—no, need—to know what happened, and very often these stories provide a staging ground for profound reflection and the communication of important values.

It would seem that adults are not so different—even though they have learned to disguise their desire to know the remainder of the story, they are all ears during the children's story in church. Some of the best teachers we had in school were those who could tell a good, gripping story. Jesus Himself was a master storyteller. His parables, a particular subspecies of a story used to teach one or two major points that are not necessarily based on a particular happening, were powerful teaching tools that disarmed enemies bent on His destruction, spoke to a wide gamut of people coming from different walks of life, and opened the way to profound theological reflections.

Throughout history stories have played an important part in people's lives, and they continue to do so. You most likely picked up this volume because you are interested in the stories of some of the shadow figures of Scripture.

So, what is the link between story and history? Can we rely on texts that are clearly well-structured and thought-through literary masterpieces? Do these books describe a historical fact or a theological reflection of a different reality? Scholars have raised these questions and have come to often widely differing solutions. As you read this book, we hope to provide you with an introduction to narratives and helpful definitions and examples of terminology that may enrich your personal study of Scripture and its hundreds and hundreds of stories. Finally, we will provide a quick overview of biblical history relevant to our shadow figures. In broad strokes we hope to provide you with a useful backdrop to help you examine each biblical character in their specific context, thus helping you to see them as real people.

Story and History: What's Happening?

Since the enlightenment period and the rise of rationalism, scholars have questioned the historicity and validity of biblical stories. The past 150 years have witnessed an increasingly accelerating challenge to biblical history, leaving Christians wondering if one should really put one's eggs into this seemingly "holy" basket of biblical authenticity. The effects of Charles Darwin's publication of the *Origin of Species* are still felt today. The debate about creationism and evolution is heated and has reached the inner sanctum of the Seventh-day Adventist Church and its impressive educational system. The implications of accepting Darwin's hypothesis for a Bible-believing Christian range from having to relegate Genesis 1 and 2 to the status of nonhistorical legends or myths that have only some vague theological significance to the obvious question about the relevance of worshipping God on the Sabbath—especially if Creation did not occur in seven literal, 24-hour days.

Following the "demise" of Creation, critical scholars began to question the authenticity of the patriarchal period, suggesting that all the stories about Abraham, Sarah, Isaac, Jacob, and the rest of them did not really contain historical facts, but were—you guessed right—just "stories."[1]

Story and History: The Bigger Picture

The issue of the link between story and history is closely associated with the much bigger issue of how one reads Scripture. Is this just another ancient (and extremely well-preserved) text containing stories that may or may not have happened at one time, or is this the Word of God, communicated by human authors using their own writing skills, styles, artistry, and experiences?

Most modern scholars would opt for the first perspective while Seventh-day Adventists would clearly subscribe to the second viewpoint. After all, *all* Scripture is inspired by God (2 Tim. 3:16, 17), and this divine inspiration guarantees the historicity of the Bible.

German Protestant theologian Ernst Troeltsch (1865-1923) formulated three important principles of historical-critical scholarship at the end of the nineteenth century that are still foundational for those who suggest a deep divide between story and history.[2] *First*, according to Troeltsch, history is a closed system ("principle of correlation") that has no space for supernatural intervention that cannot be verified after the event. *Second*, since all historical events are homogeneous, they must be understood in terms of our present experience and condition ("principle of analogy"). Troeltsch would most likely ask where one could see divine intervention in current world history and politics, which then becomes the basis for suggesting that biblical history, which contains many references to divine intervention, should rather be understood as myth or a theological or ideological take on the reality of the biblical author. *Third*, Troeltsch suggested that the most basic approach to research and history should be a critical perspective ("principle of criticism"). This, in turn, leads to tentative or probable reconstruction, but never to assured or absolute perspectives.

After this heavy, but brief, dose of German philosophy and theology, it is easier to understand critical scholars who make a distinction between something that is told with a specific purpose in mind (i.e., story) and something that happened in a particular verifiable way (i.e., history). But does this distinction make sense, especially when we recognize, as current linguistic studies have done, that language is not "objective" and value-free but carries many nuances that are not easily recognized in their meaning (semantics), forms (morphology), and structure (syntax)? Does this "critical" approach not place the criteria of the modern reader or researcher as the highest measure of authenticity, thus giving the ultimate authority over the text to the reader?

Bible stories (and history) always reek of (or at least hint to) the divine presence on this planet. Since the worldview of the people living in Bible times had more space for God and was less compartmentalized, their written accounts were full of God. God spoke to individuals and congregations (Gen. 16:13; Jer. 35:17); God fought for His people (Joshua 10:42); God instructed on issues ranging from lifestyle (Lev. 19:19) and construction (Ex.

25:8), to clothing (Lev. 19:19; Deut. 22:11) and the choice of marriage partners (Deut. 7:3). He truly wanted to be part of the life of His people.

This does not mean that biblical history and stories are always complete, giving us the whole picture. They are selective, often focus on individuals instead of nations, and sometimes have gaps covering centuries. (The gap between the death of Jacob in Genesis 50 and the birth of Moses in Exodus 2 is roughly 300-plus years). All this is due to the fact that each story has a specific purpose that goes beyond the writing of a complete history: the historical accounts in the Bible tell the story of God's immense grace, love, and, yes, justice in dealing with humanity.

In an age of political correctness, biblical history and stories are unabashedly interpretive. The events described in the Bible are from the perspective of the Lord: Noah finds favor in the eyes of God in a time when the earth is ripe for judgment (Gen. 6:8); the Lord deals with the selfish intentions of the builders of the tower of Babel (Gen. 11:3-8); and God converses with Moses regarding the comportment of the people and their construction of the golden calf (Ex. 32:7-14). The reader—ancient and modern—is drawn into the story and looks at events and the processes leading to these events through the eyes of the divine "Author" of the text.

Discovering the Beauty and Artistry of Biblical Storytelling

Literary texts, such as stories, require a sense of the involved literary artistry. Ideally, every modern reader of the Bible would be able to read the stories in their original languages (Hebrew, Aramaic, and Greek), which would greatly help to catch the beauty and careful design of biblical literature. The biblical authors, after having received the divine revelation, did not just sit down and write. Awed by the great task of communicating God's will and purpose for His people, they must have sat down and carefully planned their words. Some of them were well educated (e.g., Isaiah, a member of the royal family whose literary mastery is quite obvious—even in English); others may not have had the privilege of spending many years at "university."

Unfortunately, we do not live in an ideal world, and very few of us read the original languages. However, much of the literary design and form of biblical texts is evident in the different translations that we use in English, Spanish, German, or any other modern language. The key issue here is that we recognize that—as any prudent high school student writing an essay for a language class—we need to pay attention to the building of plots in literature, which we will briefly introduce in the next section.[3]

14

Plot

Plot can be defined as the succession of events that finally lead to a conclusion. This succession is often motivated by conflict or tension. Plot is the connection of all relevant parts of the story, which together make up a whole. A plot helps to structure a story and organize it. However, plots are often multidimensional or show different strands. The book of Jonah tells a seemingly simple story: a renegade prophet of God tries to flee from his divinely appointed task and, after many detours finally ends up doing the job that God had wanted him to do in the first place. This simplistic reading of the plot is correct, but it is not the entire story. Jonah is also a story of God's interaction with a wayward creation, beginning with a prophet who should be on the side of God and ending with the people of Nineveh who truly cross the line to God.

Character(s)

Characters of a narrative are closely connected to the plot of the story. The understanding of the character is controlled by the narrator who may even be one of the characters (as, for example, in Daniel 1). Characters can be "flat" or "round." A flat character is usually not very complex and is used to describe one particular trait or element. A round character is complex and multidimensional and is much more like a real person. The amount of information that they supply determines the development of the characters, often including conscious gaps in the development of the character. The modern reader needs to pay close attention to every detail that can be gleaned from the text about the character(s), because biblical stories tend to be very concise.

A good example of the differences in characters can be found in the story describing the miraculous birth of Samson (Judges 13), which involves three different characters: Manoah (who is the only one with a name in the story), his nameless wife, and the angel of the Lord. The contrast of the two human protagonists (another term used to describe the character) is evident:

> "In the contrast of characters a thematic statement about religious experience is developed. There is the man, Manoah, who must have a name, must be sure, must map out the future, must fit his experience to the norms and expectations of ordinary social life and the standard rules of religion. There is the man's wife, 'the woman', who is deprived of a name, yet who is blessed in her bar-

renness, knows a divine word when she hears it, trusts God, and is satisfied to ask (or presume) no more. There are two ways of relating to the divine. They seem to be related not just to the particular man, Manoah, and the particular woman, his wife, but perhaps also stereotypically to 'man' and 'woman.'"[4]

Setting

Settings impart reality to the narrative and create atmosphere and mood. Settings fall into three types: physical, temporal, and cultural. For example, when Boaz convenes his legal case in the city gate and not in his home or in the house of the main elder of the city of Bethlehem, he is acting within the culture and custom of his time. The author of Ruth is conscious of this practice and physical and cultural settings converge. Obviously, the gate, being the "most public" place in ancient times, adds an important legal (and not just romantic) aspect to the story. Setting can also indicate a time period in which the narrative unfolds and can structure a story. As another example, the "ups" and "downs" of Israel's relationship with the Lord are reflected in the going up and coming down of Moses on Mount Sinai (Ex. 19-32).

Point of View

The point of view of the story is intimately linked to the narrator who controls the story. It is their perspective through which we see the unfolding story, providing us with important information about a character or keeping that information from us. Generally, we can distinguish between first- and third-person narratives. In a first-person ("I" or "we") perspective, the narrator is part of the story—for example, Nehemiah refers to "we" in his confessional prayer (Neh. 1:7). The angle that the narrator provides shapes our reaction to the story. In many instances the Bible contains statements that evaluate a given situation: "Now the men of Sodom were wicked and were sinning greatly against the Lord" (Gen. 13:13, NIV). This point of view or commentary is designed to provide the reader with additional information, helping to take sides.

The Basic Outline of Israel's History: A Crash Course

In this section we will briefly describe the basic outline of Israel's history as it is relevant for our study of the shadow figures in this volume. Note the concentration of people associated with the time of David (Jonathan, Rizpah, Joab, Abiathar, Uriah, and Abigail). This is by no means accidental, but rather it is a reflection of the importance of David and his lineage in the history of God's people in the Old Testament. This outline is based on the biblical data itself and will link it to the larger political context of the ancient Near East.[5]

The Exodus event is one of the most important moments of biblical history and is central to the book of Exodus. First Kings 6:1 provides an important anchor for the chronology of this period, indicating that the construction of the Temple in the fourth year of Solomon occurred 480 years after the Exodus. This can be dated between 970-966 B.C.,[6] which would date the Exodus around 1450-1446 B.C. It is noteworthy to consider the el-Amarna letters, written in cuneiform at the beginning of the fourteenth century B.C. by various kings of the Canaanite city-states to the Egyptian pharaohs Amenhotep III and IV, which contain the call for help of these city rulers to the Egyptian king against an unknown group called the *habiru*. If the Exodus occurred around the middle of the fifteenth century B.C., the settlement period would begin around the beginning of the fourteenth century. This is the time of Joshua and Caleb who were also part of the Israelites leaving Egypt 40 years earlier (Joshua 14:7-10).[7] The biblical books of Joshua and Judges describe this period and the subsequent period of the judges which is one of the darkest moments of Israelite history or continuous ups and (more) downs. Hannah lives toward the end of this period, which lasted approximately 350 years.[8]

Following the settlement period and the period of the judges, Israel clamored for a king (1 Sam. 8). The biblical books describing the early history of Israelite monarchy are 1 and 2 Samuel. Samuel acts as the unwilling kingmaker and counselor for the first king of Israel. The length of Saul's reign is difficult to determine since the Hebrew text of 1 Samuel 13:1 seems to be missing some crucial information. The New International Version follows some manuscripts of the Septuagint (the Greek translation of the Old Testament) while a literal translation of the Hebrew would be: "Saul was a year old [lit. the son of a year] when he became king, and he reigned over Israel two years." Obviously, Saul was much older than a year when he was anointed by Samuel (1 Sam. 10:1). Concerning the length of his reign, the only other biblical statement can be found in Acts 13:21, which contains a reference to 40 years, even though we should note that the Greek text does not contain the verb "to reign" in the verse.

David's reign begins around 1010 B.C. as king of Judah in Hebron (2 Sam. 2:1-7), followed by his coronation over all of Israel some seven years later (2 Sam. 5:1-5). After 40 years (counting from his reign over Judah),

Solomon is crowned in order to avert a coup d'état by Adonijah (1 Kings 1). Solomon's reign is marked by stability, prosperity, and enormous public building programs, including the Temple, his palace, and numerous fortification systems in Israel. While this period appears to be the golden age of Israel from the outside, Solomon's heavy reliance on corvée labor (i.e., compulsory, unpaid labor demanded by a lord or king) sows the seeds of rebellion and the later division of the kingdom (1 Kings 12:4). Solomon's reign also lasted 40 years (1 Kings 11:42), and by 930 B.C. the 10 northern tribes rebel against Solomon's son Rehoboam and Israel separates from Judah.

The history of the northern tribes is characterized by rebellion against God, syncretism (just remember the rival shrines in Bethel and Dan that Jeroboam I established), court intrigue, and numerous dynastic changes. By 722 B.C. Israel is absorbed into the Neo-Assyrian empire and the inhabitants of Samaria and the surrounding regions are exiled to Assyria. The nameless man of God, the widow of Zareptah, and Gehazi live (or minister) in Israel and fall into this historical period.

The southern kingdom is continuously governed by David's descendents, even though there is also a constant coming and going of faithful and rebellious kings. After seemingly endless calls for repentance and change by numerous prophets, Judah is also allowed to fall into the hands of its enemies, and in 586 B.C. Nebuchadnezzar, king of Babylon, captures the city after more than two years of siege, destroying its fortification system, palaces, and the Temple of the Lord and marching its inhabitants into exile to Babylon. Baruch, the secretary of Jeremiah, lived through these tumultuous times and is the last protagonist of this volume.

The Basic Outline of This Volume

After this atypical introductory chapter, the next 12 chapters will follow a more structured outline. Each chapter will begin with an *Imagine . . .* section, which will introduce the character in a creative (and sometimes surprising) way. In *Meet the Cast* we will introduce the key characters of the story, which is followed by the *Background Information* section, which contains relevant cultural, linguistic, or historical information. The fourth section of each chapter is titled *Action* and focuses on the basic story line. The main part (in terms of quantity) of each chapter is the *Digging Deep* section, which will choose one particular Bible passage to analyze within the context of the story. *Issues* tries to biblically answer some questions or challenges arising from the story. Finally, *Reaction* features blog-like entries by us that will hopefully encourage you to interact personally with the story.

[1] John van Seters (University of North Carolina) and Thomas Thompson (recently retired from the University of Copenhagen, Denmark) are two scholars who have repeatedly and consistently challenged the historicity of the patriarchal period: John van Seters, *Abraham in History and Tradition* (New Haven, Conn.: Yale University Press, 1975); idem, *In Search of History* (New Haven, Conn.: Yale University Press, 1983); or Thomas L. Thompson, *The Historicity of the Patriarchal Narratives* (Beiheft zur Zeitschrift für die alttestamentliche Wissenschaft 133; Berlin: de Gruyter, 1974); idem, *The Origin Tradition in Ancient Israel*, Journal for the Study of the Old Testament Supplement Series 55 (Sheffield: JSOT Press, 1987).

[2] Helpful volumes dealing with key issues of the interpretation of the Bible (or hermeneutics) from an Adventist perspective include the following: George W. Reid, ed., *Understanding Scripture: An Adventist Approach*, Biblical Research Institute Studies 1 (Hagerstown, Md.: Review & Herald, 2005) and Gerhard F. Hasel, *Biblical Interpretation Today: An Analysis of Modern Methods of Biblical Interpretation and Proposals for the Interpretation of the Bible as the Word of God* (Lincoln, Nebr.: College View Printers/Biblical Research Institute, 1985). Focusing especially upon the method of reading the Pentateuch compare also Gerald A. Klingbeil, "Historical Criticism," in *Dictionary of the Old Testament: Pentateuch*, ed. T. Desmond Alexander and David W. Baker (Downers Grove, Ill.-Leicester, U.K.: InterVarsity Press, 2003), pp. 401-420.

[3] Some helpful references for further in-depth reading include the following: Robert B. Chisholm, Jr., "History or Story? The Literary Dimension in Narrative Texts," in *Giving the Sense;* David M. Howard, Jr., and Michael A. Grisanti, ed., *Understanding and Using Old Testament Texts* (Grand Rapids, Mich.: Kregel Publications, 2003), pp. 54-73; Yairah Amit, *Reading Biblical Narrative: Literary Criticism and the Hebrew Bible*, trans. Y. Lotan (Minneapolis, Minn.: Fortress Press, 2001); Walter C. Kaiser, "Narrative," in *Cracking Old Testament Codes: A Guide to Interpreting Literary Genres of the Old Testament*, ed. D. B. Sandy and R. L. Giese, Jr. (Nashville, Tenn.: Broadman & Holman, 1995), pp. 69-88 (most chapters in this volume are very helpful for those seeking to understand the literary dimensions of the biblical text); or Lee J. Gugliotto, *Handbook for Bible Study* (Hagerstown, Md.: Review & Herald, 1995), pp. 33-71.

[4] David M. Gunn and Danna Nolan Fewell, *Narrative in the Hebrew Bible*, Oxford Bible Series (New York, N.Y.: Oxford University Press, 1993), p. 67.

[5] A very helpful history that takes seriously the biblical data and integrates it with extrabiblical data is the following book: Iain Provan, V. Philips Long, and Tremper Longman III, *A Biblical History of Israel* (Louisville, Ky.-London, U.K.: Westminster John Knox Press, 2003). We based the concise outline on their comments.

[6] Scholars recognize that there was a time of coregency between David and Solomon, since David was still king when Solomon was crowned (1 Kings 1:28-40). David's death is reported in 1 Kings 2.

[7] The 40 years of wandering in the wilderness are amply documented in the biblical text. Compare, for example, Joshua 5:6 or Nehemiah 9:21. Concerning the historicity of the settlement and current scholarship, consult the following book: Richard S. Hess, Gerald A. Klingbeil, and Paul J. Ray, Jr., eds., *Critical Issues in Early Israelite History*, Bulletin for Biblical Research Supplements 3 (Winona Lake, Ind.: Eisenbrauns, 2008).

[8] The total number of years of oppression and rulership by the different judges comes to 410 years plus the undefined period of Shamgar (Judges 3:31). Seeing that between the end of the settlement (around 1400 B.C.) and the early reign of Saul (around 1050 B.C.) are only 350 years, it is most likely that some of the periods of oppression or rulership were parallel, perhaps covering different locations.

Chapter 2

Caleb:
Living With the Wait

Imagine...

Caleb's Obituary in the Hebron *Times*:
We are saddened to announce the death of Caleb son of Jephunneh. Today we have lost a truly great man—a father in Israel.

Caleb of the tribe of Judah was born into slavery in Goshen, Egypt. Caleb's childhood and youth were spent in dreary drudgery, working on various Egyptian building projects. He, together with our people, was able to leave Egypt and slavery in a dramatic rescue maneuver now known as the Exodus, which ended in a high-speed chase and the decimation of the Egyptian army at the Sea of Reeds.

Although never really an up-front type of person, Caleb's undeniable leadership skills led to his life-changing nomination as the official Judah delegate on a daring espionage mission in occupied Canaan. Upon returning from the mission, he, together with Joshua son of Nun, valiantly tried to avert a national disaster after the other 10 delegates falsified reconnaissance reports.

Caleb most recently made headline news by actively leading, at the age of 85, a military operation against the giant Anakites. Although a great national leader, he will be remembered as a humble, generous, kind, and faith-filled man. He will be greatly missed by his sons Iru, Elah, and Naam, and his daughter, Acsah, and son-in-law, Othniel. He will be buried on his own land at Hebron. More specific funeral plans will be announced in due course.

Meet the Cast

Caleb: The meaning of his name is uncertain, but it is associated with the Hebrew term for "dog." In the ancient Near East dogs were generally not regarded highly, and there are numerous references to the pejorative use of the name ("raving dog" or "dead dog," etc.). However, the faithfulness of a dog is also documented in different extrabiblical sources. Caleb's faithfulness and trust in God's power is one of the motifs that shines through the story of his life.

Joshua: He followed Moses as the leader of Israel. Together with Caleb, he was one of the 12 spies that checked out the land of Canaan. Joshua and Caleb were the only people over 20 years of age who had left Egypt and were allowed into Canaan. He died at 110 years of age (Joshua 24:29).

Moses: He is perhaps the greatest Old Testament character, and he is the author of the majority of the first five books of the Bible.[1] In ancient times the first five books of the Bible were known as the five books of Moses. The name "Pentateuch" (simply indicating a five-part book) came into use in the second century A.D.[2] This would mean that the first references to Caleb were recorded by Moses, himself one of the central figures of the Exodus.

Other Ten Spies: These men, who are reported by name in the Bible, were leaders of their tribes and were chosen to represent their tribe in the spying mission to Canaan. Considering the impact of their report, they must have been good public speakers. After presenting their factual report, they began to sow fear and mistrust by leaving God out of the equation and stating that Israel was not able to take the land of Canaan (Num. 13:26-33). They seemed to have been caught up in the feeling of the moment, and between them and the crowd they whipped themselves up into a frenzied state. They moved from the factual to the illogical, contradicting themselves by stating that the land "flow[s] with milk and honey" (Num. 13:27, NIV) but "devours those living in it" (verse 32, NIV). They suffered the consequences of their lack of faith in God and died of a plague (Num. 14:37).

Acsah: The daughter of Caleb, Acsah was most probably born during the 40 years the Israelites camped out in the desert. An eligible young woman, she served as incentive for the conquest of Kiriath Sepher, and she married her cousin Othniel (Joshua 15:16, 17). After she was married she made an unconventional request of her father, who gave her water springs in the Negev (verses 18, 19).

Othniel: The son of Kenaz, Othniel was Caleb's nephew and later son-in-law. He was a young warrior who led in the conquest of Kiriath Sepher and won Acsah's hand in marriage. Years later he was used by God to deliver the Israelites from Cushan-Rishathaim, king of Aram Naharaim. He became Israel's first judge (Judges 3:7-11).

Anak's Sons: Ahiman, Sheshai, and Talmai were leaders of a group of original inhabitants of Canaan who lived in the area of Hebron. They seem to have been very tall and strong-looking people. The sight of them, more than anything else, drove fear into 10 of the spies who then claimed that they felt like "grasshoppers" (Num. 13:33) in their presence and that the Israelites stood no chance against them. In a great show of faith, Caleb asked for this territory, and as one of the two oldest men in Israel, he conquered the giants that had scared an entire generation of Israelites.

Background Information

Caleb lived through momentous times, including the Exodus from Egypt, the prolonged wanderings in the desert, as well as the early days of the settlement period in Canaan. Based on the chronological reference in 1 Kings 6:1, Caleb was born some time in the early fifteenth century B.C. This was a time of great international developments. Beginning in the New Kingdom time period, Egypt began to extend its influence into Canaan in order to create a buffer zone against another invasion from the north that had traumatized Egypt during the Second Intermediate Period when the country had been dominated by foreign rulers known as the Hyksos.[3] The division of Egyptian rulers into dynasties is due to the work of the Egyptian priest Manetho who lived during the third century B.C. and wrote a history of Egypt in Greek. The most important dynasties of the New Kingdom in Egypt were the eighteenth and the nineteenth dynasties. A fifteenth century B.C. date for the Exodus would place this important event in the life of Caleb and the people of Israel during the reign of the eighteenth dynasty.

Egypt's influence in Canaan is documented by the extrabiblical letters from el-Amarna that were discovered in 1887. These diplomatic communications, originating in Canaan and sent by the rulers of small Canaanite and Syrian city-states to pharaohs Amenhotep III and IV in the fourteenth century B.C., contain urgent requests for help against individuals or groups described as *habiru* that were attacking their cities. While the Israelites were not exclusively the *habiru* (who are also known in much earlier texts from the eighteenth century B.C. and have been linked to people or individuals "outside of the law"), they may have been part of that group. Clearly, as invaders, they were considered "lawless" and aggressors.[4]

Surprisingly, the letters were written in Akkadian (not Egyptian hieroglyphs), which highlights its importance as the international language of commerce and diplomacy. Besides the correspondence with the Canaanite or Syrian vassals of Egypt, the archive also contained letters documenting the Egyptian relations to the other major international powers of this time, including the Babylonians, the Assyrians, the Mitanni (a Hurrian-speaking group located in northern Syria), and the Hittites.

God's timing for His people was impeccable. Considering the international political landscape at the end of the fifteenth/beginning of the fourteenth centuries B.C., the superpowers of its time (such as Egypt, Assyria, or the Hittites) were absorbed in internal problems, leaving Canaan unprotected, so that Israel would have to conquer only the local population and did not have to deal with the much larger threat of one of the regional superpowers.

Action

Although Caleb is only a shadow figure and not a main character, his story is interwoven with a larger section of the biblical narrative. Caleb's story probably begins somewhere in Exodus 2 and ends in Judges 1. Caleb's life was action-packed. He witnessed and was part of the birth of a nation. He began life as a slave in Egypt, and he vividly experienced firsthand the power of God in the 10 plagues. Assuming that he was a firstborn[5] child, the blood on the doorpost of his house saved him on the terrible night of deliverance when the angel of the Lord passed over the homes of Egypt, destroying all the firstborns not covered by the blood of the lamb.

He took part in the greatest escape in history as the Israelites left Egypt loaded with the treasures of their captives. Caleb ate manna, camped at the foot of Mount Sinai, and heard God's voice as the ground shook and the mountain exploded. He looked on in disgust as many of his countrymen, soon after hearing God's voice, danced around a golden calf. Caleb embarked on the long journey to the borders of the Promised Land.

Although the first 40 years of Caleb's life were quietly lived in relative obscurity, Caleb was observing, learning, remembering, and cultivating a relationship with God. This gave him the moral strength to make his mark on history after the exploration of the land of Canaan. He was ready, prepared, and convicted to speak out, to go against the popular verdict and encourage others to have faith in God. In spite of his faith in God, he, along with all those who disbelieved, spent the next 40 years wandering in the desert, facing water shortages, snakes, revolts, and the Israelites' frequent faith meltdowns. Finally, he stood again on the border of the Promised Land. As one of only two remaining from his entire generation,

Caleb did not retire to a well-earned rest, but rather, he led in the conquest of the land with a new generation.

Although he led by example, he did not cling to his leadership position and feel threatened by younger people. Rather, he looked for creative ways to nurture their faith and leadership. There was no artificial divide between Caleb's public and private life. The last action we hear of in the Bible is an insight into Caleb, the family man. In Joshua 15:19 Caleb generously gives his daughter (who would not be legally entitled to any of his property) not only land (which would be lost to him and his family, seeing that his daughter was integrating into the family of her husband) but also water rights (which is one of the most precious commodities in the dry Middle East).

Digging Deep

In this section we will look at Caleb's first recorded words, which can be found in Numbers 13:30. Although this is only one short verse, we will have to look at what comes before and after Caleb's speech in order to put his words into context.

Numbers 13 begins with God's command to explore the land of Canaan. The Israelites are camped on the borders of the Promised Land, and leaders of the different tribes are chosen to join the spy expedition. Since this is an official mission, each chosen representative is first introduced in the context of his tribe. He is then mentioned by name, followed by the father's name, which indicated a person's clan and had a similar function as a last name in modern times.

Numbers 13:16 mentions that Moses gave Hoshea the name Joshua. Renaming was often done by a leader to show a great change or new commission or role that a person was being given. "Joshua" is particularly significant as this would be the Hebrew form of Jesus and means "the Lord is salvation," a fitting name for a leader who would face tremendous odds. The fact that Caleb does not get a new name emphasizes his shadow role. He is not being called to a visible leadership position.

In Numbers 13:17 the spies get their orders. This is not a vacation sightseeing trip. The spies are called to do a research project; they have research questions and are to go in search of the facts. God encourages data gathering, surveys, fact-finding missions. Our Christian experience should not be marked by a lack of personal research or superficial scanning. As individuals we are encouraged to search the Bible[6] individually and as a community of believers.

Numbers 13:26-29 is a factual report of the results of the fact-finding mission, even though one can note tendentious comments in some places, such as the "but" that opens verse 28 (NIV). Facts need interpretation in order to be relevant. Here Caleb speaks out and takes the initiative in the interpretation of the facts. He sees a great land that God has given to the people. The 10 other leaders leave God out of the equation; all they see are giants. As we look at the facts of our lives, our present world, or even science and history, we will come to vastly different conclusions depending on whether or not we are interpreting the facts with or without faith, and including God in the equation.

Words are powerful. The 10 spies with their faithless report had no idea how far-reaching their words would be or what their report would lead to. The change is dramatic and sudden; the vast crowd's mood changes from an excited expectant atmosphere to one of extreme disappointment, despair, and anger. The words of the spies seem to have an effect on the speakers themselves, and they extend their story to include illogical statements, not based on fact. If the land was so bad (verse 32) that it swallowed up those in it, how was it that it could also nurture giants?

In chapter 14 we see the effect of the report. The ugly mood grows in the camp, and people are ready to actually go back to Egypt.[7] Moses and Aaron plead with God. Caleb and Joshua do not keep quiet, and they try to stem the tide. This is incredibly brave. Imagine standing up to a big crowd of angry people who seem to have turned off their memory and rationale. Both Caleb and Joshua are passionate about the truth, and they cannot just stand by and watch the nation be misled. Numbers 14:6-9 documents their speech. Although it does not indicate who did the talking, it would seem that both of them spoke. Their actions of tearing their clothes indicate the depth of their feeling.[8] They are just two men willing to speak out for God in a seething mass of people who, like hooligan supporters of the team that lost, are looking for victims to take out their rage on. The crowd is beyond reason and seeks to stone Caleb and Joshua were it not for God's direct intervention in verse 10.

The last time Caleb is mentioned in the book of Numbers is in chapter 14, verse 24, where God singles him out for special mention! Joshua will become a leader and a very visible character, but God wishes to reinforce the truth that He notices the "little" people. God knows that a different spirit—namely His Spirit—lives in Caleb, and even in his unassuming way Caleb is following God wholeheartedly. God will reward his faith and trust. He alone of all that generation will enter the land of Canaan.

Issues

Numbers 14:18 has caused some Bible readers some discomfort. Especially within an individualistic twenty-first century mind-set, we see justice as a personal thing in which the guilty person "pays" for what they have done. We have come a long way from the reality of community. Like it or not, in a very real sense, all our lives are entwined and all our choices affect others as well as ourselves. We consider the idea of children suffering the consequences of the sins of their parents as unfair and unjust. The way God views issues of justice, punishment, and group, as well as individual, responsibility is beautifully highlighted in the story of Caleb. In Numbers 14:10 God steps in and stops the Israelites from stoning the leadership and now Moses is mediating with God on behalf of an undeserving community. He quotes God's own words back to Him[9] and includes the difficult words of verse 18, which state that "he does not leave the guilty unpunished; he punishes the children for the sin of the fathers to the third and fourth generation" (NIV).[10]

How does an application of this principle play out in the life of Caleb and his Israelite community? First of all, we can see that God is patient. This is the tenth time that the Israelites have rebelled against God's leadership (Num. 14:22).[11] There are consequences for disobedience. Sometimes consequences for sin can be delayed, but inevitably, the consequences will have to be faced. Because of the Israelites' continued disobedience and lack of faith, they were not allowed to enter Canaan. God told Moses that all of the generation that left Egypt from 20 years of age and up would die in the wilderness (Num. 14:29-35). Forty years of nomadic life in a dry desert would be hard. The entire community would suffer as a result of their actions, including their children (14:33) and livestock.[12]

Although we think of only two generations being affected, this punishment extends to the third or even fourth generation, as those that are near 20 years of age will have grandchildren before entering Canaan who must suffer in the desert. The sobering reality is that sin is never fair. Drunk drivers kill innocent people. In small or big ways, we all suffer from the wrong decisions of others, and in turn, we influence the lives of others and even our environment by our wrong decisions and actions. The Bible makes it very clear that there is a day of reckoning and judgment when God will actively punish individual and corporate sin,[13] but much of what we suffer is a consequence of our own or other people's sins.[14]

Caleb gives us hope for escaping this cycle. Although the community made the wrong choice, he stood firm and tried to turn the tide. Even though his voice did not seem to make a difference, God noted it. While he had to suffer along with the innocent children and waste the best years of his life in the wilderness, God had not forgotten him. The special promise to Caleb (Num. 14:24) is a promise to all of us who are victims of the consequences of sin in our world. God has not forgotten us. He will sustain us and ultimately reward our faithfulness.

Re-action

Chantal: I find a lot of myself in Caleb. I think I am generally more of a behind-the-scenes kind of person, but in one aspect, I think I am very different from Caleb. Caleb was prepared to stand out and stand alone if necessary. I am someone who prefers to avoid conflict at almost any cost. I have a wonderfully supportive family and friendship circle, but would I have the moral strength to stand by faith and trust in God if all those I love and appreciate were talking gloom and distrust? I want more of the Spirit that lived in Caleb to enable me to know when to quietly observe and when to stand out.

Gerald: Patience is not one of my strengths. I wish I had the stamina that Caleb showed when he waited for more than 40 years for the fulfillment of God's promise. I wish I had the long-suffering character Caleb exhibited when he walked away from the borders of the Promised Land for another 38 years of nomadic living, knowing full well that this was not his fault. I don't see any finger-pointing in Caleb's life. He is not the type of individual to find the guilty party and make sure they know that it is *their* fault. He shows a great deal of solidarity, something I could also use more of in my life.

---

[1] Moses could not have written Deuteronomy 34 because it describes his own death.

[2] Compare John H. Sailhamer, *The Pentateuch as Narrative*, Library of Biblical Interpretation (Grand Rapids, Mich.: Zondervan, 1992), pp. 1, 2.

[3] The history of Egypt is complex and has to deal with large amounts of material, including numerous texts and archaeological and iconographic data. A very helpful and readable volume, written by one of the foremost current Egyptologists that links Egypt to the history of Canaan, is Donald B. Redford's *Egypt, Canaan, and Israel in Ancient Times* (Princeton, N.J.: Princeton University Press, 1992).

[4] If you would like to read more about the el-Amarna letters, you can consult the helpful summary by Nadav Na'aman: "Amarna Letters," in *Anchor Bible Dictionary*, 6 vols., ed. David Noel Freedman (New York, N.Y.: Doubleday, 1992), vol. 1, pp. 174-181. A good translation of the Akkadian texts can be found in W. L. Moran's *The Amarna Letters* (Baltimore, Md.-London, U.K.: Johns Hopkins University, 1992).

Illuminating Shadow Figures in Scripture

[5] The fact that Caleb was chosen as the representative of Judah in Numbers 13:6 would suggest his firstborn status (as well as his leadership qualities) in a society and culture where age and birthrights were important.

[6] The Bereans were highly commended because they did not accept any teaching without first comparing it to the Scripture they had (Acts 17:11).

[7] Some 38 years later, Moses tells this story to the next generation, who were probably too young to remember it or had not been born yet (Deuteronomy 1:19-36). Notice that Caleb is mentioned in this abbreviated version, too.

[8] Tearing of clothing was mostly associated with mourning or coming face to face with bad news. Compare Genesis 37:29 (Reuben tears his clothes when he sees that Joseph is not in the pit), Joshua 7:6 (Joshua tears his clothes when hearing of the rout at Ai), and 2 Samuel 1:11 (David and his men tear their robes when they hear of the death of Saul and his sons).

[9] In Exodus 34:6, 7 God shows Himself to Moses and states the verse that Moses quotes back to God in Numbers 14:18.

[10] See, for example, the discussion in the following publication: Gerald A. Klingbeil, "Between 'I' and 'We': The Anthropology of the Hebrew Bible and Its Importance for a Twenty-First Century Ecclesiology," in *Bulletin for Biblical Research,* 19 (2009), pp. 319-339.

[11] Remember that these people had seen the 10 plagues in Egypt and walked through the parted Sea of Reeds. And yet they continued to choose unbelief. See, for example, Exodus 15:22-26; 16:1-20; 17:2-7; 32:1 (the golden calf episode took place right after having heard the voice of God); and Numbers 11:1-7.

[12] Similar examples of consequences affecting generations of individuals can be found in the Old Testament record, including David's sin that resulted in the death of David's first child from Bathsheba and his subsequent family problems (2 Sam. 12:14–20).

[13] God expects "undiluted loyalty" and promises "loving kindness" to a "thousand (generations) of those who love me and keep my commandments" (Ex. 20:6, NIV). The contrast between three or four generations and a thousand is marked and deliberate, emphasizing the unlimited response of God to those who love him, but the limited punishment of those who disobey reaches the third and fourth generations.

[14] For another difficult example see Joshua 7. As a result of Achan's sin, his larger community suffered, including his immediate family, his animals, his tribe, and the confederacy of tribes, representing Israel as a people.

Chapter 3

Hannah:
Learning to Be Someone

Imagine...

Hannah's story is such an intimate story. Join us for an imaginary interview with this special woman.

Question: "Hannah, how important are children in your culture?"

Answer: "My whole culture revolves around children. After all, we are the children of Israel! When God, long ago, made a covenant with our forefather Abraham, the promise was all about children. He vowed that we would be as numerous as the sand on the seashore or the stars of the heaven and that we would be given this land as an inheritance forever. I think each of us sees ourself as part of a living chain, stretching from God's promise to Abraham, down through the generations into Egypt, through the wanderings in the desert, and then into the Promised Land. This living chain stretches on through us into all the future generations who share in the covenant. Each family has a share of the land as we also share the promise of God. So, you can imagine that a couple without children to pass the land on to is a terrible fate. Imagine that after all these generations the chain stops with you? You have failed miserably at the most important thing in life. You have broken the living chain of God's promise to Abraham for all generations. Besides this, there are also the everyday practical questions. Who will work the land when we become too old? Who will support us in our old age?"

Question: "On a very personal level, Hannah, tell us how it feels to be barren?"

Answer: "I feel so useless. I have failed Elkanah. What comes so naturally to everyone else does not come to me at all. All my friends started having children, and soon, I was the only one left without a baby. I was not a part of their world anymore. They were awkward around me. Each month my husband looked at me with anxious expectancy, and I had to shake my head. Eventually he took another wife. I cried myself to sleep that first night. Even though Elkanah was kind and loving toward me, things were never the same. Soon Peninnah gave birth to a child, underlining the fact that I, and not my husband, had been the problem all along. And I thought that I had been unhappy until then—that was the beginning of the real agony for me! Peninnah has a thousand ways of telling me in looks, intonation, and private conversations, which she wants me to overhear, that I am not wanted. I am a stranger, an outsider, even an enemy in my own home. All I really have to hang onto is God, and yet I often wonder . . . why has God made me barren? Is this a punishment for some hidden sin? Does He not consider me worthy to be a part of the covenant people, to continue the blessing? Am I outside of His love?"

Meet the Cast

Hannah: In Hebrew the name Hannah means "favored grace," which is ironic considering her barrenness. She is a gentle patient woman who has endured years and years of provocation and self-doubt without becoming hard or bitter. Her faith in God—a God that for many years she could not see actively working on her behalf—makes her the character to watch in this story. She is also a poet and uses her gift to eloquently praise God. She is one of a number of biblical characters who could not conceive naturally and yet had a miracle child.[1] Perhaps because of the circumstances of their birth, these children were anything but ordinary. In Hannah's case her involvement with Samuel did not end with her giving him to the Lord or even when he left home.[2] Hannah daily wrapped him in prayer as she prepared something practical for him each year.[3] Hannah was richly rewarded for the gift she gave God. God gave her more children (1 Sam. 2:21).

Elkanah: His name means "God has created/taken possession." The biblical author provides us with an extensive genealogy for Elkanah, which helps to establish his pedigree, provides a historical anchor and reality to the story (after all, these facts can be checked by the reader), and tells us about important roots. The genealogy also insinuates what will be lost if there is no heir. In 1 Chronicles 6:27 and 34 it suggests that he was most likely a Levite living in the territory of Ephraim, which would make Samuel's service in the tabernacle even more legitimate. Elkanah tried to keep the peace in the two-wife household, but he was also a victim. Similar to Abraham and Sarah, he is a good example of somebody taking things into their own hands—he takes a second wife.[4] He is committed to the worship of the Lord and faithfully attends the annual pilgrimage to the tabernacle. He is also supportive of the vow that Hannah makes, since a vow of a married woman had to be ratified by her husband.[5]

Peninnah: Peninnah is the character in this story that transforms a sad situation into a bad situation. When she enters the home of the childless Elkanah and his first wife Hannah, she produces children but is not content. She specializes in making Hannah's life miserable. Even during the most solemn religious festivals, she continues to terrorize Hannah.

Eli: Eli represents a contrastive character. He should have been one of the most powerful, effective leaders in Israel, but in reality he was weak and ineffective. He shows a gentle tender heart like Hannah and seems to be controlled by his parental love, leading to overindulgence with his sons (1 Sam. 2:29). He opts for the nonconfrontational approach in child rearing. Even though the worship of God was the center of his life, his children had effectively become his idols.[6] He stands in stark contrast to Hannah who is willing to give her long-awaited, much-loved son to God and His service even though that means she can see him only once a year.

Samuel: Samuel is the youngest character in the story and makes his appearance only halfway into the story of Hannah. Nonetheless, he is a very important person. He is a living testimony to the fact that God hears our prayers. Samuel's life demonstrates that worship is not only for adults. The child Samuel serves and worships God. He learns to serve God and participate not only as a spectator but as a participant in worship. The Bible reports that "the boy Samuel continued to grow in stature and in favor with the Lord and with men" (1 Sam. 2:26, NIV), which is later echoed by the description of Jesus' childhood (Luke 2:52).

Background Information

The time period between the Israelite settlement in Canaan and the coronation of the first king covered about 350 years. It was a time of darkness and light, ups and downs, and it showed a repetitive pattern: Israel would forget God's law and His mighty acts of the past, worship idols and be overrun by one of their powerful neighbors. At rock bottom they would turn to God and plead for help. God would raise up a judge to liberate them and lead them back to God. As soon as the generation of the judge died out, the next generation would turn back to idolatry and the cycle would begin again.

The last judge known prior to the arrival of Eli had been Samson, the strong weak-man. Although he had brought Israel a moment of reprise, killing many Philistine leaders during his last act of judgment, there was no true revival. Israel was in religious, political, and social chaos. Everyone did exactly what he wanted to do (Judges 17:6). The worship of God was compromised. Eli's sons were "scoundrels" (1 Sam 2:12, NLT), and those officiating at the tabernacle seemed to have forgotten what sacrifice was all about and thought only of their own gain. No central authority in the person of a strong judge was on the horizon. Things looked dismal for Israel.

Action

The plot of this story seems at first glance to be fairly simply. It is not a great action-packed plot involving kings and decisive battles that will change the course of history. This is the story of a harassed childless woman who prays for a child and then, on receiving the long hoped-for child, does the most amazing thing of returning her child to God. And yet, this simple story tells us about God's view of history. While we may think that big names doing big things is what makes history, the story of Hannah shows that the patterns of our everyday, regular, ordinary lives are not insignificant. Our lives, our problems, our longings are important to God. Each of our lives—even the seemingly insignificant ones—is woven into God's great tapestry of history and will bear significant fruit in the light of eternity. This childless woman with her personal pain and then sacrifice had no way of knowing that the son she gave to God would become a great prophet and judge who would leave his unmistakable mark on the course of Israelite history.

Probably because this is an ordinary sort of life lived by ordinary people, most of the action involves ordinary comings and goings. Movement between the hill country of Ephraim and the tabernacle frames the story (1 Sam. 1:3). This is a singular beginning for a biblical book. Although the book will focus on great national and international movements, the story begins on a very personal and intimate level as it focuses on a desperately sad, barren wife. We are quickly drawn into the movement of the life of this family, which takes us to the tabernacle. Faced with Peninnah's constant provocation and a seemingly silent God, Hannah begins to pray. Her prayer is so vivid that Eli assumes that she is drunk. The good news for all of us is that God's action is not confined to His tabernacle. God acts at home, and Samuel is born. We then join Hannah, little Samuel, and Elkanah on their way back to the tabernacle where Hannah will sing her wonderful song of praise. Hannah moves in this story from being a victim to being a victor.

Digging Deep

In this section we will focus on the song of praise that Hannah sings as she brings young Samuel to the tabernacle. Making music in biblical times was not linked to commercial enterprise, where people collaborated to produce an album that needed to be released on a certain date. Most biblical songs were not commissioned, but rather, they were created in response to a particular life circumstance. Many of the singers (and thus the authors of the songs) were women.[7] The context of Hannah's song is sobering: she is bringing what she always wanted, a child, to be left behind in the sanctuary under the care of an old man and his wicked sons who "had no regard for the Lord" (1 Sam. 2:12, NIV)—and yet she is singing.

Her song is really a faith psalm, looking beyond the visible to see the invisible—a world turned upside down. Hannah's song is full of military imagery, which echos the great controversy theme. The song begins and ends with the Lord raising a horn. The animal horn was often used in poetry as a symbol of strength (Ps. 18:2; 148:14).

1 Samuel 2:2 emphasizes the fact that God is incomparable and unique. This is a time of national idolatry. Even most Israelites probably thought of God as *one* among many gods. Hannah realizes that God is not like the other gods. God is not bound to a particular place or function. God is not obliged to play the game by our rules. Rather, we are invited to come and unlearn the rules of life as it is commonly lived and relearn to view life from God's perspective. We are invited to come and take refuge in the Rock. As a description of God, the rock symbolizes protection, strength, and even has messianic significance.[8]

Verse 3 begins with a warning against pride and arrogance. These attitudes show that the speaker has no idea of who she is dealing with and just how great God is. One of the first things we need to realize in God's presence is the need to be honest. There is no point in trying to impress God. He knows us and, even more, what our motivations are; by Him "deeds are weighed" (verse 3, NIV).[9]

Verse 4 begins with a military image. Perhaps one of the most feared members of an army were the bowmen. A powerful barrage of arrows could stop an advancing army. However, here we have the reversal of the image. Superior firepower means nothing to God. He can simply break the bows of the warriors. And those that are stumbling and are almost down, He can arm with strength. Very often God's answer is not a sudden show of superior firepower but rather an impossible persistence that He gives to His people (Isa. 40:31; 42:3). Perhaps one of the greatest miracles God per-

33

forms in us is our ability to keep going in the face of trials or difficult life circumstances as we keep drawing on God's strength. God's strength is made perfect in our weakness as we let God shine through our brokenness.

From a war image Hannah's song now moves to another time of crisis, i.e., famine or drought (verse 5). People who have always had things going their way now find themselves in dire straits and have to hire themselves out for basic food.

Some of the humiliation of the situation Hannah sings about and the role reversal can be found in the story that Jesus tells a thousand years later of a well-to-do young man who never thought too much about the basics, such as, what he would be eating. This young man goes to a foreign land, wastes his money, and then finds himself in a famine and becomes so desperate that he hires himself out to a farmer to look after the pigs. He is so hungry that he contemplates eating the pigs' swill (Luke 15:13-17).

In Hannah's song those who have been hungry are no longer hungry—God satisfies them. Perhaps they are like the prodigal son who comes home to a totally underserved feast, or perhaps they are like one of the shocked poor, blind, or lame that are taken to the king's banquet instead of the rich and well connected who have no need of the king's feast (Luke 14:21).

From hunger and feast Hannah moves to perhaps the most personal part of her song. The many years of being barren and the accompanying shame that the barenness brought must flash through Hannah's mind as she sings of a woman who was barren and now has borne seven children. Hannah, at this point, has only one child, and she is at the tabernacle to give her miracle child to the Lord, but she has tasted the miracle—God has worked in her life. She chooses the number seven (often indicating perfection in Scripture) to depict the completeness of God's doings. The Lord has given the barren woman the perfect or complete number of children, while the woman that seemed to have it all in contrast (verse 5 tells us that she had many sons) pines away. She may have many sons, but the happiness, security, and honor that this is supposed to bring eludes her because it is not given by God.

Verse 6 reemphasizes the way Hannah views her world. God is all-powerful, and He is in charge. For a modern reader the beginning phrase of the "Lord brings death" may sound very strange. We generally think of death as being something that Satan brings, but for Hannah and the ancient Hebrew mind-set they saw no difference between what was permitted and what was actively done. In other words, if God has the power to stop something and yet permits it to happen, then God is seen as having done it. Notice how the Lord uses the negative things of life to teach something, and then when the lesson of dependence on Him is learned, He delights in seating the poor and needy with princes and letting them inherit thrones of honor. Reversal is one of the key terms of Hannah's story. Hannah seems to understand that a life lived with God is not all plain sailing, but that pain has a purpose and ultimately there will be heaven. Nobody can be saved and go to heaven because they earned it; rather, the saved will know that they are the prodigals rescued from the pigpen.

Hannah's song moves on to a reaffirmation of God's authority as Creator and Judge (verses 8-10). Hannah realizes that the only way to live is to choose to be on God's side. She knows that choosing to be on God's side will bring wonderful rewards in the future, but she also realizes that everyday life with all its role reversal can only be successfully lived by God's strength. For all the powerless victims Hannah's song brings good news that justice will prevail. The prophetic Messiah, the anointed King,[10] the just Judge of all the earth, will be coming.

Hannah's song is particularly pointed as she sings it in the time of judges where the wicked seem to get away with murder and even the best seem to be flawed. Perhaps Hannah's world is a lot like our world. Perhaps we, too, can sing in God's strength as we wait for ultimate justice to prevail.

Issues

The biblical worldview does not divorce fertility, children, or family from religion and worship. However, unlike the prevailing concept of its time, the Bible does not categorically make infertility a punishment by God for something.[11] It is clear that God can cause infertile people to bear children. In the biblical record, when someone is directly kept from having children by God it is always because God is planning a special birth and wishes to highlight the event and person by making the conception and birth something out of the ordinary.[12]

Perhaps the whole issue of infertility can best be seen in Jesus' answer to His disciples concerning a man born blind. Blindness, like infertility, was believed to be the direct punishment by God for individual sins. The disciples asked Jesus who had sinned: the man, who had been blind from birth,[13] or his parents. Jesus answered, "Neither this man nor his parents sinned, but that the works of God should be revealed in him" (John 9:3, NKJV). Infertility then does not seem to be an issue of God punishing an individual or a couple. Infertility was not part of God's original plan, but like blindness, birth deformities, cancer, or HIV, these diseases/defects remind us that we live in a sinful world. Yes, sometimes these conditions are consequences of choices, but who is to blame did not seem to interest Christ and should not interest us either. Where the disciples saw problems, Jesus saw possibilities. God's power can be shown in our lives, and He promises to make our lives rich, fertile, and fulfilling whether or not we have children.

Re-action

Chantal: Hannah's life makes me look at my world with new eyes. Society seems to tell me that, as a woman, I need to be thin, young, beautiful, and a top businesswoman or have an academic degree to have worth. I find it wonderful to be reassured that I don't have to have an academic title to be someone special. I don't have to claw my way to the top of anything to find my worth. Hannah found her worth in God, and so can I. God hears my prayers and answers!

Gerald: I am amazed at Hannah's commitment to her promise. As a father I would have thought twice to send my child into an environment that was obviously not safe and spiritually uplifting (1 Sam. 2:12-17). How often do I rationalize my way out of a commitment I have made? I wonder if a glimpse behind the curtain dividing this earth from the heavenly realm would help me trust more in the power and might of a loving and caring heavenly Father? When was the last time I saw God's supremacy and control of my circumstances so clearly that I could just break out in song and rejoice in the God who holds the universe in the palm of His hands? When was the last time it happened to you?

---

[1] See, for example, Sarah (Gen. 16:1; 17:17), Rebecca (Gen. 25:21), the wife of Manoah (Judges 13:2), and Elizabeth (Luke 1:7).

[2] This happened, most likely, around the age of 4 years when Samuel was weaned (1 Sam. 1:23, 24).

[3] Ellen G. White tells us that "when separated from her child, the faithful mother's solicitude did not cease. Every day he was the subject of her prayers. Every year she made, with her own hands, a robe of service for him; and as she went up with her husband to worship at Shiloh, she gave the child this reminder of her love" (*Patriarchs and Prophets*, p. 572).

[4] We should not be too hard on him though. Taking a second wife in the case of barrenness of the first wife was the cultural norm of his time. However, the household conflict underlines the fact that cultural norms, outside of God's plans, result in unhappiness.

[5] According to Numbers 30:10-15, a husband had a veto right over his wife's vows. Note the interesting link to vows; in 1 Samuel 1:21 it states that Elkanah went to worship

every year in order to fulfill a vow; however, we are not told what the vow was for. According to the test in Numbers, Elkanah only had to be silent on hearing of his wife's vow in order for it to be valid. Elkanah is more than silent and confirms her vow in 1 Samuel 1:23.

[6] His fondness for his sons made him turn a blind eye even when they were openly desecrating and bringing shame on the worship of God (1 Sam. 2:12-17).

[7] Miriam leads the women of Israel in song after they witness God's incredible power and protection at the Red Sea (Ex. 15:20, 21). Her song is some type of response to Moses' song (Ex. 15:1-19). Mary's "Magnificat" has been the focus of numerous composers and authors (Luke 1:46-55).

[8] See, for example, Deuteronomy 32:4; Psalm 118:22; Isaiah 28:16; Matthew 21:42; Mark 12:10; Ephesians 2:20; and 1 Peter 2:4. Cf. Samuel Terrien, "The Metaphor of the Rock in Biblical Theology," in *God in the Fray: A Tribute to Walter Brueggemann*, ed. Timothy K. Beal and Tod Linafelt (Minneapolis, Minn.: Fortress Press, 1998), pp. 157-171.

[9] This revelation of what is really in me leads to the reaction of Job when he met God: "Surely I spoke of things I did not understand, things too wonderful for me to know. . . . My ears had heard of you but now my eyes have seen you. Therefore I despise myself and repent in dust and ashes" (Job 42:3-6, NIV).

[10] Ellen G. White states that "Hannah's words were prophetic, both of David, who should reign as king of Israel, and of the Messiah, the Lord's Anointed" (*Patriarchs and Prophets*, p. 572).

[11] The only exception seems to be the case of Michal, David's wife—although, it is not clear if the judgment pronounced by David was an indication that God was actually punishing her with infertility or if David was not sleeping with her anymore.

[12] See, for example, Sarah, who at the age of 90 eventually bears Isaac, the son of the promise given so many years earlier, or Rebecca, who is able to conceive only after special intercessory prayer and then gives birth to twins. Compare also the stories of Rachel, who is loved but barren—she eventually gives birth to Joseph and Benjamin—or the wife of Manoah, who gives birth to the judge Samson after the visit of an angel. In the New Testament we know of Elizabeth, the mother of the greatest of all prophets—John the Baptist—who was the forerunner of Jesus Himself.

[13] This is what puzzled the disciples. A newborn could not have a chance to sin, yet why would he be punished? If his parents had sinned, then why did the blind man have to bear the blame?

Chapter 4

Jonathan:
Born for Greatness

Imagine...

Imagine Jonathan's journal entry before the battle at Micmash . . .

"The situation looks pretty desperate. We did expect the Philistines to come with a chariot force. We were hoping to push the battle into more rugged terrain to give us an advantage. We definitely did not expect them to show up with 3,000 chariots and at least 6,000 charioteers. We haven't been able to get an estimate on the enemy soldiers numbers—they seem to be as numerous as the sand on the seashore.

"The Philistines have already sent out three raiding detachments. One seems to be heading for the vicinity of Shual. The other toward Beth Horom, and the third is already overlooking the valley of Zeboim. The main military strategy behind these raiding detachments seems to be to force the main battle location into an area in which they can make full use of their chariot force. A secondary strategy seems to be to destroy the morale of our troops. The Philistines have been very successful. We have had a record number of desertions this past week. Our men seem to be melting into caves, thickets, rocks, pits, and cisterns.

"By the last count, we had only 600 men left. Looking at all of those armor-clad Philistines reminds me of how poorly equipped we are. My father and I are the only ones with proper armor and swords. Everyone else is armed with gardening forks, sticks, or axes. Militarily speaking, we have no chance.

"Some might think I'm crazy, but I believe we will win. We have God! God always specializes in impossibilities. I believe that God will act on our behalf. Nothing can hinder the Lord from saving, whether by many or by few. Perhaps God is waiting for someone to take the lead, someone to step out in faith. There is that Philistine detachment right here at the pass at Micmash. I wonder . . ."

Meet the Cast

Jonathan: His name means "Yahweh has given," and as the first son of King Saul, his parents (like any Israelite parents) must have rejoiced over his arrival. Jonathan is the first in the list of Saul's sons (1 Sam. 14:49). Jonathan's claim to fame is due to his selfless character and his complete trust in the God of Israel. When faced with an overwhelming enemy at Micmash, Jonathan is ready to step out in faith—against all odds and reason (1 Sam. 13:2–14:46). He makes a good role model as someone who balances both loyalty to one's origin and the friendship that may require stepping out of one's comfort zone and making difficult choices. Jonathan's friendship with David is a wonderful example of selfless commitment (1 Sam. 18:1).[1] Jonathan dies with Saul in battle on Mount Gilboa fighting the Philistines. The Philistines then expose the bodies of Saul and his sons on the wall of Beth Shan (1 Sam. 31:1-13). In a daring night raid, the inhabitants of Jabesh Gilead rescue and burn the decomposing bodies and bury the bones in Jabesh.

David: David is one of the main characters of the Old Testament. His name may be a shortened form of "Beloved by [Yahweh]." He is the eighth son of Jesse of Bethlehem (1 Sam. 16:1-13) and a valiant warrior (1 Sam. 17). When he marries Michal, the daughter of King Saul, he becomes not only the king's son-in-law but also Jonathan's brother-in-law. David is anointed secretly by the prophet Samuel while the previously anointed king is still in power. Saul's jealousy drives David to flee the royal court, and he becomes the leader of a band of battle-hardened warriors that seem to have fallen foul of Saul's regime (1 Sam. 22:1, 2). Once David gains (at least partial) control of the kingdom, he energetically sets out to establish regional hegemony, making Jerusalem as the new capital (2 Sam. 5:6-16) and subduing the surrounding tribal groups.

Jonathan's armor-bearer: No name and origin are given; however, he plays an important role in Jonathan's miraculous defeat of the Philistines at Micmash. His response to Jonathan's daring invitation to attack the better positioned Philistine garrison somehow echoes Jonathan's own selflessness and deference toward David (1 Sam. 14:7).

Saul: He was the first king of Israel and father of Jonathan, belonging to the tribe of Benjamin. His name means "one requested, asked for." Chosen by God to reign over Israel (1 Sam. 9-11), Saul at first celebrates important military victories, but due to his neglect of the Lord's commandments (1 Sam. 13:13; 15:14-23), he is finally rejected by God, and David is secretly anointed by the prophet Samuel. As the first king of Israel, chosen during a time of national distress, Saul focuses primarily upon military concerns over nation-building.

Philistines: During the late period of the judges and the early years of the monarchy, the Philistines, located mainly along the coastal strip of Palestine, are the archenemy of the Israelites. They are organized as a confederation of cities, including five major cities: Ashdod, Ashkelon, Ekron, Gath, and Gaza. Archaeological data suggests a close link to Aegean culture, possibly via Cyprus.

Background Information

Jonathan and David's story is a story about two families. Clan and tribal loyalties were still highly relevant during the early days of the monarchy. The kingship had not yet developed into what we imagine as royal power—particularly considering the long history of powerful European royal courts prior to the Enlightenment Period.

Israel's first kings did not have an established capital and felt most at home (and supported) in their ancestral homelands (1 Sam. 10:26). The anointing of David while Saul was still officially the divinely appointed king created tensions and jealousies among the two involved parties (1 Sam. 16:1-13). Saul's demise is counterbalanced by David's amazing rise. David becomes the champion of the people due to his military prowess and leadership (1 Sam. 18:5-7). Naturally, this displeases Saul (1 Sam. 18:8, 9), particularly considering the fact that there was no established history of kingship in Israel at that time, and thus, military leadership appeared to be the key qualifier for Israelite kings.

David's years of living as a fugitive from Saul, including also his hideout in Philistine territory (1 Sam. 27), highlight again the important element of clan and/or tribal relations. As can be seen in contemporary examples from tribal societies, loyalties and alliances are of a somewhat tentative nature and can change from day to day, depending on the current situation and necessities. Saul's obsession with defeating David underlines his diminishing sense of God's presence in his life and the life of Israel. God's Word is not relevant anymore to Saul, since it does not fit into his own scheme of things.

Action

Jonathan truly is a protagonist who does not claim the limelight. His most heroic exploit involves attacking single-handedly a Philistine outpost at Micmash. In this apparently foolhardy enterprise, Jonathan is supported by his young, loyal armor-bearer. In order to understand the action a bit better, it is helpful to pay close attention to Jonathan's dialogue with his armor-bearer in 1 Samuel 14:6-10. This passage showcases Jonathan's belief in Yahweh, not as a clan deity or a god needing to be pacified through sacrificial offerings but as a God who was personally involved in the affairs of Israel. Jonathan's active faith in divine providence and leading marks a major difference from his father, Saul. Later on, David seems to demonstrate a similar depth of faith and the recognition of divine providence in his encounter with Goliath (1 Sam. 17:37).

Undoubtedly, Hebrew readers of the narrative would quickly catch the link between the hoped-for action in 1 Samuel 14:10, "the Lord has given them," and Jonathan's own name, which means the same. The choice of the sign is ironic; an affirmative divine sign will actually be Jonathan's marching orders. As they step out of their hiding place into the viewing field of the guards, the Philistines react as hoped for, and Jonathan and his armor-bearer advance, killing twenty enemies in their advance. Panic ensues[2] and the earth quakes—earthquakes were considered a sign of divine intervention (see 1 Sam. 7:10) and often linked to theophanies, divine appearances (see Judges 5:5; 2 Sam. 22:8; and Ps. 29). While Jonathan and his armor-bearer were truly brave, the biblical author wants to communicate to the reader that God—again—was acting as the divine warrior, fighting for His people.[3] The resulting victory for Israel is of God's doing, not of Jonathan's doing.

Jonathan's most unselfish act is the moment when he recognizes David's divine call. Here, he differs starkly from his father, Saul, who seems to cling to his throne and position. By protecting David's life and establishing a covenant with him, Jonathan consciously steps aside from his own ambitions and dreams (1 Sam. 20). Saul recognizes their friendship and angrily throws insults at Jonathan (verses 30, 31), but this does not seem to make any difference to Jonathan, which demonstrates how close their friendship was. Verses 16 and 17 link the legal implications of covenant relationships (which is also visible in other nonbiblical ancient Near Eastern texts) with the concept of love. However, Jonathan and David's love goes beyond political loyalties and expediencies and involves genuine friendship. It is action that speaks louder and lasts longer than any military conquest. This action is risky as it nearly costs Jonathan his life when his irate father throws a spear at him (verse 33).

Digging Deep

How do we determine God's will for us in specific situations? As Christians this is where our faith really plays out in everyday situations. In this section we will look at how Jonathan figured out that it was God's will for him to attack the Philistines at Micmash (1 Sam. 14:1-14).

To begin with, Jonathan understood *who* God was. This was not a test to see if God existed. Jonathan had absolute trust in God. Jonathan was utterly sure that God can save. "Nothing can hinder the Lord from saving, whether by many or by few" (verse 6, NIV). He is not trying to manipulate God or force His hand—rather, Jonathan wants to find out how he fits into God's plans. Jonathan has the right attitude. He is prepared to accept God's will; he was not trying to use God's will as a pretext to do his own will or force someone else into his plans. In verse 9 he makes it clear that he is prepared to stay and "not go up to them" if God so indicates. Ellen White cautions us to "exercise wisdom and judgment in every action of life, that we may not, by reckless movements, place ourselves in trial. We are not to plunge into difficulties, neglecting the means that God has provided, and misusing the faculties He has given us."[4]

John Wesley adds to this thought by warning, "do not hastily ascribe things to God. Do not easily suppose dreams, voices, impressions, visions, or revelations to be from God. They may be from Him. They may be nature. They may be from the devil. Therefore, believe not every spirit, but 'try the spirits whether they be from God.'"[5] The Bible warns us to "not believe every spirit, but test the spirits to see whether they are from God" (1 John 4:1, NIV). We are also told to "test everything" and "hold on to the good" (1 Thess. 5:21, NIV). This testing begins with finding out what Scripture has to say about something. God always acts in harmony with His revealed will in the Bible.

We can often predict what others will choose or say if we know the person. The closer we are to the person the easier it becomes to know what they will do or want, even in a new set of circumstances. As we become better acquainted with the Bible, we will be better able to know what God wants us to do in a new situation. Jonathan had only a very limited portion of the Bible compared to what we have, and yet, he knew that God had called and established Israel and had promised to fight for them and save them if they turned to Him for help. This knowledge of God's bigger plan helped Jonathan to define better what God wanted for him that day at Micmash.

Sometimes the line between faith and presumption can seem very fine. Jonathan understands that God is not limited. He does not try to manipulate God into doing what he wants. Instead, Jonathan looks at the circumstances to find out if they are providential. He is willing to stay or go; the important thing is that Jonathan is waiting on God to reveal His will through the sign that he proposes.

Likewise, we also need to look at the circumstances surrounding us and find out if they are providential. Is the Lord speaking to us through events or people in our lives? This is where we may need to ask for a sign.

It is important to note that Jonathan does not depend on his own impressions exclusively. He consults with another God-fearing person and confides in him his plans and ideas (1 Samuel 14:6, 7).

Finally, Jonathan gets the go-ahead. Jonathan can say in absolute faith and assurance "Climb up after me; the Lord has given them into the hand of Israel" (verse 12, NIV).

Issues

Friendship involves a mutually beneficial relationship between people. That's a good scientific definition. Friendship, however, is usually not clinical and sterile. It involves emotions, may cause pain, and requires continuous work and commitment. Sometimes the relationship between God and a human being is described in terms of friendship. Abraham is called God's friend (Isa. 41:8; James 2:23). Moses, speaking face to face with God, "as a man speaks with his friend" (Ex. 33:11, NIV), is another example of divine-human friendship.

In the New Testament Jesus illustrates this divine-human friendship even further. After all, He is the incarnated Word, the Creator of the universe. God's friendship is not only reserved for the good and the deserving (those who do not need a physician, Matt. 9:12), but Jesus seeks out the marginalized, the lonely, the sinners (such as prostitutes and tax collectors)—people that most of us would make a big circle around. In His high-priestly prayer Jesus links being a friend to keeping the commandments (John 15:14)—not as a means of salvation but rather in terms of imitating Jesus' love and focus on community ("as the branch remains in the vine").

Friendship is also closely linked to identity. I can be a good friend only if I know myself and am capable of loving and accepting the ugly parts of my character. Loving my neighbor as myself is one of the key principles of friendship (Lev. 19:18). Jesus builds on this important concept and expands it to include not only friends (or those we find easy to love) but also our enemies (Matt. 5:43, 44). Understood in this light, Jonathan's friendship must have grown out of a deep recognition of who he was as a person. He must have found his place in life, even though it may not have been in the palace in Gibeah.

Being unselfish is definitely out of fashion these days. Giving up a seat to a woman in a full metro car or bus can be construed as acting paternalistic or chauvinistic—at least in the United States. Again, Jesus is our role model. He, "who, being in very nature God, did not consider equality with God something to be grasped, but made himself nothing" (Phil. 2:6, 7, NIV), became a servant in order to serve humanity. Jesus is indeed someone to be emulated. Beginning with the stable in Bethlehem and moving to the carpenter's hut in Nazareth, the divine master plan for the incarnation included no royal palaces and red carpets. Instead, Jesus was called to mingle with pushy and smelly crowds, touch the unclean, and serve the undeserving.

The Communion service is a good illustration of this principle of unselfishness. As the disciples bicker about who will get the prized spots next to Jesus (for the feast, but also in the soon-to-be-established kingdom), Jesus takes off His outer garment, stoops down to pick up the basin and the towel, and begins the seemingly demeaning task of washing dirty and smelly feet. Michael Card has captured this scene in a most wonderful way:[6]

> In an upstairs room
> A parable is just about to come alive.
> And while they bicker about who's best,
> With a painful glance He'll silently rise.
> Their Savior Servant must show them how
> Through the will of the water
> And the tenderness of the towel.

And the call is to community,
> The impoverished power that sets the soul free.
> In humility to take the vow,
> That day after day we must take up the basin and the towel.

Re-action

Chantal: Jonathan's life demonstrates to me the importance of supporting roles. I guess I sometimes feel that if I am not president or cofounder or manager of something important then perhaps I am not that important.

44

Sometimes introducing myself as a homeschooling mom sounds so unexciting, especially after having been a professor at a seminary. Jonathan shows me that striving to be in a more visible position is not what heaven views as greatness. A rock-solid faith, warmth, and loyalty radiate from Jonathan's life as a friend and son. I want the same faith, warmth, and loyalty to shine from my life as a daughter, wife, and mother.

Gerald: Friendship seems to be a dying species, at least in our predominantly Western context. People have become expendable and sacrifice has the feel of a four-letter word. Do you still remember your best friend from school or college? Do you still keep in touch? Have the sometimes shallow and bewildering communication styles of Facebook and Twitter replaced the moments of intimacy that face-to-face talking and sharing used to create? Jonathan-style friendship is a unique gift, and I am glad for all my friends that have often surprised me with their loyalty and devotion. I wonder, though, how capable am I to give of myself unselfishly? Or am I just busy "counting the costs" without acting on them?

---

[1] Some scholars have suggested that David and Jonathan's friendship was more than a healthy male friendship. However, this perspective seems to be a rereading of a story situated in the Iron Age of the ancient Near East in the light of conventions and concerns of the twenty-first century. While Jonathan "loved" David (1 Sam. 18:1), so did Judah and Israel (1 Sam. 18:16) and Saul and his servants (1 Sam. 18:22).

[2] The Hebrew root translated with "trembling" or "fear" is the same as the one used in 1 Samuel 13:7 where it describes (ironically) the reaction of the Israelites when faced with the powerful Philistine army. Now, the tide has turned. It is the Philistines' turn to tremble and fear.

[3] Compare Ralph W. Klein, *1 Samuel*, Word Biblical Commentary, vol. 10 (Dallas, Tex.: Word, 1983), p. 136. The divine warrior motif is very important in Scripture. See, for example, Martin G. Klingbeil, *Yahweh Fighting From Heaven: God as Warrior and as God of Heaven in the Hebrew Psalter and Ancient Near Eastern Iconography*, Orbis Biblicus et. Orientalis, vol. 169 (Fribourg/Göttingen: University Press/Vandenhoeck & Ruprecht, 1999) and T. Longman III and D. G. Reid, *God Is a Warrior*, Studies in Old Testament Biblical Theology (Grand Rapids, Mich.: Zondervan, 1995).

[4] Ellen G. White, *The Desire of Ages* (Mountain View, Calif.: Pacific Press Publishing Association, 1940), p. 369.

[5] As quoted by James Dobson, *Emotions: Can You Trust Them?* (London, U.K.: Hodder and Stoughton, 1980), pp. 119, 120.

[6] Michael Card, "The Basin and the Towel," on *Poiema* (Sparrow, 1994).

Chapter 5

Abigail:
No Victim of Circumstances

Imagine...

A bigail's **Practical Guide to Crisis Management**
   1. Listen: A lot of crises can be completely avoided by listening. Ideally, form a network of people who will be honest with you. Your network should not be just your friends or peers. Listen to people on the ground. I personally find listening to my servants very helpful. Be an approachable person. Let people speak without interrupting them.

2. Define your problem: In a time of crisis, rationally defining the problem may be difficult, but it will be essential to your survival. In my case I realized that the threat to my household was based on the facts that David and his men needed food and that David had been insulted.

3. Take stock of your resources: Part of any crisis is normally the time issue. You have to look at what you have on hand to meet a crisis. Normally, there is no time to order provisions or obtain help from outside sources. You will have to make do with what you have physically and/or emotionally. Although it is impossible to have all the resources available for any emergency, it is wise to keep the basics. Keep physically fit by regular exercise and maintain a good diet. Keep spiritually fit by regular prayer and worship times. Memorized Scripture will prove one of your greatest resources in a time of crisis. To meet my crisis, I had bread, wine, sheep, grain, raisins, and figs on hand that could be given to David's men.

4. Formulate a plan: Be willing to take the initiative and take the lead, if necessary. Do not let social conventions stand in your way. In my culture a woman does not normally manage a rescue mission. Of course, this is not the time to fight the status quo or make a point. Even if you have a good point to make, in a crisis it is important to be humble and flexible and let God use you.

5. Look at the big picture: During a crisis it is very easy to focus on the problem and our own inadequacies, but as children of God, a crisis can shake us from the mundane and help us see our lives from God's point of view. Try to keep a godly perspective of the problem and encourage those involved to see consequences and possibilities.

6. *Debrief:* After the crisis has passed, take time to debrief (with those involved, if possible) and learn from the experience. Tact will be needed to select the correct time for debriefing. I had to wait until the following day to tell my husband what had happened.

7. *Things to avoid:* During a crisis or the debriefing, avoid blaming, accusing, or threatening others.

Regardless of where our crises come from, God wants to use them to help us grow as we learn to depend on Him.

Meet the Cast

Abigail: Her name could be translated as "my father rejoices," which may be possibly a reference to a special moment in her family associated with her birth. Abigail is introduced into the biblical narrative as the wife of Nabal, the Calebite (1 Sam. 25:3). She is described as being wise, which she demonstrates in her quick actions and appraisal of the situation involving David and his men.

After the sudden demise of her "foolish" husband, Nabal, Abigail becomes David's wife and is mentioned together with the Jezreelite Ahinoam several times in the following chapters (1 Sam. 27:3). Both of David's wives are captured by the marauding Amalekites (1 Sam. 30:5) and later liberated by David and his men during a dramatic rescue operation (1 Sam. 30:18). After David's coronation in Hebron by Judah, Abigail gives birth to David's second son, Chileab (2 Sam. 3:3, KJV). Since neither Abigail nor her son appear again after the Hebron years, it is possible that they may have died during that period.

Nabal: In Nabal's case the Latin dictum of *nomen est omen* (the name is an omen) is a sad reality. Nabal means "fool," and foolishness (coupled with rudeness) seems to have been one of his main character traits—at least according to the brief character description found in 1 Samuel 25. Nabal is a Calebite, i.e., he belonged to the clan that was founded by Caleb. As a wealthy sheep owner, he lives in Maon and tends his sheep and goat herds around the town of Carmel. There is no mention that he and Abigail had children. While Nabal feasted and drank (1 Sam. 25:23-36), his wife saved the day by organizing a delegation that brought provisions to David and his men.

David: While there are no specific time references, David's persecution by Saul takes a significant space in 1 Samuel, covering over a third of the entire book. This is a formative period of David's life, and the ups and downs and uncertainties of his personal life are a good reflection of the uncertain nature of the early Israelite "state," which was experiencing external and internal pressures. While Saul is increasingly obsessed with securing his throne by getting rid of David, his rival, David, is portrayed as protecting towns and communities that are exposed to the Philistine threat—in 1 Samuel 23 David saves Keilah, and in chapter 25 he saves Nabal and his household.

Throughout his trials, David has to be careful of whom he trusts. Loyalties are not always clear and often shift according to political realities on the ground. In 1 Samuel 23 David delivers Keilah, but when faced with the possibility of Saul's assault on the city, David learns that the elders of Keilah plan to hand him over (1 Sam. 23:12). This is typical for tribal communities lacking a clear national identity and a strong central power. Faced with Nabal's insults, David's reaction is understandable and even justified, but Abigail points out in 1 Samuel 25:26-28 that, as a king, David must look beyond personal and clan pride toward a bigger national community. He must also let the Lord fight his battles.

Background Information

The chapter detailing the intriguing story of David, Nabal, and Abigail is bracketed by two chapters hinting at David's greatness. Twice he spared Saul's life. In 1 Samuel 24 David cuts off a corner of Saul's robe (verse 4) while the Israelite king uses a cave, where David and his men are hiding, as a restroom. In 1 Samuel 26:8-12 David and Abishai do not succumb to the temptation to kill Saul with his own spear. As circumstances would have it, the hunted suddenly becomes the hunter. In both stories David highlights the sacredness of the Lord's anointed, even though cutting off the corner of a garment was not such an innocent act as twenty-first century readers may think.[1] David seems to recognize this and immediately regrets this actions (1 Sam. 24:5-7). Clothing did not only make a person, as Swiss author Gottfried Keller once wrote ("Kleider machen Leute") but in the ancient Near East it was thought that clothing itself could actually be equivalent to the person. In Mesopotamia the hem of a person's garment could be used in the person's absence as a means of authentication.[2]

Sandwiched between these two stories, we find the triangle of David, Nabal, and Abigail. This story portrays David realistically not as a saint (in the common sense of the word) but as an individual that can, at times, react emotionally and flawed when put in the right or wrong circumstances. In other words, David looks like us.

The description of the property of Nabal marks him not as a subsistence farmer but as a wealthy landowner (1,000 goats and 3,000 sheep represented a significant amount of wealth). As already evidenced in the previous chapters, David and his 600 men are constantly on the move, and during the shearing season he sends 10 young men to the wealthy landowner to request a gift of recognition for the protection given to Nabal's men during the past season by David's forces. David's request should not be seen as a mafia-style shakeup for protection money, but rather, his request highlights the important patronage system where the more powerful protects the less powerful and in return can expect the goodwill and recognition of the one receiving protection. The original message sent to Nabal (1 Samuel 25:6) highlights the respect that David had for the landowner (and most likely others in the vicinity as well).

Action

In a world with no central power, smaller power brokers step into the power vacuum and provide basic services, such as protection from marauding bands, tribal enemies, or even wild animals. David seems to have provided such a service to the Maon community, located in Judah, approximately 7 miles south of Hebron (Joshua 15:55).

The chapter opens with the surprising statement, seemingly unrelated to the following story, that Samuel had died and that all Israel assembled and mourned in Ramah (1 Sam. 25:1). Obviously, there is a direct link, since the death of Samuel marks the end of an era and the end of at least some sort of stability and coherence. Samuel's death also marks the hardening of the front lines between Saul and David, so David is on the move again.

His request for Nabal's "tribute" is communicated respectfully through 10 young men. Nabal's response is not only insulting but sounds like a later anti-Davidic rebel (2 Sam. 20:1). His rhetorical question, "Who is this David?" (1 Samuel 25:10), is a formal rejection of the offered covenantal agreement and is a clear attempt to cause David the "loss of face" that was so important in eastern cultures.[3] David, at least in Nabal's mind, is just a runaway servant of Saul who has big dreams but not much else. He surely must have overlooked the 600-men army that David commanded, or perhaps he felt strong enough to keep them at bay.

David's response is immediate: two thirds of his troops get ready for battle while the remainder protect the supplies. Verse 14 marks a change in the perspective of the story. Instead of focusing upon the men involved, it is time for Abigail to take center stage. An unnamed servant tells Abigail about Nabal's rudeness (and thus confirms our suspicion that Nabal's response could easily be recognized as what it was intended to be, i.e., an insult) and about the faithfulness of David's men during the past season. It is remarkable that the anonymous informer felt free to characterize Nabal before his mistress as a "wicked" man[4] without any reprimand from the mistress of the house (verse 17, NIV).

Abigail loses no time and quickly raids the barns and sheds that are filled with the supplies for the big harvest party and winter. Sending the servants and pack animals carrying the ample food supply ahead (similar to Jacob in Gen. 32:13-21), she mounts a donkey and travels right into the lion's den—with this heroic act, Abigail prevents David from acting rashly and hastily and causing bloodguilt. We cannot overestimate Abigails' action here. She, as a woman, not only negotiated directly with another man but did so with a party that were armed to the teeth and ready for action. Note, however, that most of the action described in 1 Samuel 25 is verbal and not actual.

Abigail's plan works and David's response recognizes Abigail's astuteness.

Digging Deep

In this section we will look more closely at Abigail's speech to David. But first, let's look at Nabal again. We know that Nabal was a descendant of Caleb, but he was unlike his generous ancestor who gave away not only a field but also the extremely valuable springs of water to his daughter (Joshua 15:19). All David is asking for is some provisions during the sheepshearing season when Nabal will have plenty to spare.

While David's anger over being insulted and humiliated is understandable, his impulsive action in response to this insult seems quite out of character and is more like something we would expect from Saul. God uses Abigail to bring David back to his senses and to avoid the grave pitfall of incurring bloodguilt.

Imagine David's surprise as he and his men turn a corner of a ravine and meet a train of donkeys loaded with food accompanied by a few servants and a woman who immediately bows down to him. The biblical writer repeats the bowing action in 1 Samuel 25:23 and 24. This bowing is more than just a submissive greeting. While Nabal may have asked,

"Who is this David" (1 Sam. 25:10), Abigail treats David like God's anointed, even though he is not behaving as the Lord's anointed at this moment. In the opening lines of her speech Abigail makes it clear that she is willing to take the rap. In contrast to David who chafes under baseless insult, she is ready to bear the consequences of her very foolish, unappreciative husband.

She then does something that we would not expect. She tries to get David to see Nabal through different eyes. In verse 25 she explains that Nabal's insulting behavior is not specifically targeted at David but is really just a reflection of his selfish, unhappy nature. Abigail encourages David to look past the obvious and see Nabal as someone to actually be pitied. She puts aside her own personal interests and is prepared to ask for what would be best for someone else. Abigail could have seen this threat on Nabal's life as a way of getting rid of her husband and regaining her "freedom." Instead, she chooses to identify herself with him and plead for his undeserving life.

David and Abigail's world was not so different from ours in the respect that back then everyone was just as eager to receive credit for anything that went right and escape blame if anything went wrong. We see in verse 25 how Abigail is willing to accept the consequences for her husband's bad actions, and now, in verse 26 she praises God for stopping a bloodbath rather than taking the credit for her own quick reaction. Perhaps living close to God can bring us into such a secure space that we do not feel the need to continually look out for ourselves but can live without fear of what others will think or say.

In verse 28 Abigail asks David to overlook the insult and tactfully points out two things. *First*, she reminds him that he fights the Lord's battles. Before this, David had been in the habit of asking for God's direction before undertaking military action (1 Sam. 23:2). This time there were no prayers for guidance before starting out for Nabal's house. The importance of continually and actively seeking God's will in our lives cannot be overstated. It is very easy to take a wrong turn in a moment of crisis that can have enduring consequences. *Second*, Abigail encourages David to think about the future and evaluate his actions in light of the big picture. In her statement "let no wrongdoing be found in you as long as you live" (verse 28, NIV) Abigail is obviously evaluating his character in the light of his future position as king. What sort of king would he be if he exterminated everyone he did not like? What would make him different from Saul who murdered anyone he felt threatened by?

In verse 29 Abigail again points to the big picture. In the Hebrew language the person she references is a vague "should a man," however, it is clear that both Abigail and David know that she is referring to Saul. She encourages David to contemplate God's past leading in his life. This will give him perspective for the current situation and hope for the future. In a world without zippers, valuables, such as coins, were tied into bundles that could be suspended from the owner's belt. This is a beautiful image of the security of God's care for David, and us. The second contrasting image must have taken David back to his youth as he target-practiced with his sling while tending the sheep. The object of that exercise was not to keep the stones close but rather fling them as far away as possible.

In the last part of Abigail's speech in verse 30 she shows absolute faith in God's promises. Even though the promise is made to David, she is absolutely sure that God will keep His promise. For Abigail the issue is not *if* David will become king but rather *when* he will become king.

In verse 31 Abigail reminds David that there is no handicap as difficult to bear as a guilty conscience. Perhaps she sees in her husband some of the results of living with a bad conscience. We know from David's later history how true this is. As long as David kept himself close to God and walked in God's ways, his kingdom went on from strength to strength. In contrast, after his sin with Bathsheba, everything went downhill. Even after he sincerely repented, things were never the same again.

The last part of her speech, when she asks him to remember her, seems as if she is asking him for a special favor when he becomes king. This seems strange coming from the selfless Abigail. Practically speaking, there was not much that even a king could do for a rich man's wife. Abigail is rather indicating that she is so sure of what she is saying that she wishes to be involved herself. Similarly, the thief on the cross who asked to be remembered expressed his faith in Jesus while hanging on the cross. It is easy to reassure others in a difficult or dangerous situation and remind them that God will lead them, but are we willing to become involved?

Issues

We can't read the story of Abigail and David without considering the ending. Abigail is sent for and becomes David's second or third wife (depending on whether or not we count David's first wife Michal, the daughter of Saul, who had been given to Paltiel). We could perhaps look at the story from the cultural perspective of David's day in which marrying more than one wife was a common status symbol. It would seem that all the surrounding kings had harems, and even King Saul had several concubines. Given the high infant mortality rate, this was also perhaps a way of ensuring that one would have surviving heirs.

In Abigail's case it is possible that David meant this gesture as a means of protecting Abigail and giving her a secure home. Although the Bible does not say anything implicitly against the practice of having multiple wives, the Bible keeps reminding us of all the pain, heartbreak, and negative results of polygamous families,[5] while continually holding up the ideal of one man and one woman joined together so closely that they become "one flesh" (Gen. 2:24).

For Abigail her life after marrying David was anything but the "happily ever after ending" we have come to expect from Hollywood. She too had to constantly be on the run from King Saul. At Ziklag she, along with the other men's families, was captured by the Amelekites and later rescued. And here Abigail disappears from the biblical narrative. We would all expect to see this wise and beautiful woman at King David's side playing an important role in the rest of history, and yet, there is sudden silence. The last we hear about Abigail is that she has a son named Chileab (2 Sam. 3:3), elsewhere called Daniel (1 Chron. 3:1), who was second in line to the throne by birth order, but both Abigail and her son then disappear from the record.

Many scholars believe that both she and her son died. Given the later rape, murders, revolts, and rebellions that the oldest sons were involved in, an early death was perhaps not the worst that could have happened. Every action brings a reaction. Unbeknown to David he was setting an example for his son Solomon, who would take poligamy to an extreme and be led into idolatry by his numerous wives and concubines. The idolatry that Solomon's wives introduced would never be eradicated and led to a division of the kingdom and eventually the loss of the entire kingdom of Israel. Perhaps we personally need to think through and analyze some of our modern customs in the light of the biblical ideal.

Re-action

Chantal: I am struck by Abigail's self-identity. Despite the fact that her husband was obviously not the supportive type but rather must have been inclined to put her down at every opportunity, she never lost her sense of worth. She knew God and found her security in Him. This made her proactive, creative, and tactful. As a child of God, I want to claim the same sense of worth.

Gerald: I must confess that I can identify with David's response of anger when confronted with Nabal's insulting words. I guess that is one of the reasons why God has given me my wife, Chantal, to offer wise counsel. Abigail's wisdom and her hands-on approach are good reminders that I cannot always wait for others to sort out their problems. Some situations may require a more proactive approach. In Abigail's time men usually had the final word and were supposed to sort out their differences without the input of the women-folk. I am glad that Abigail stepped out of societal norm, thus preventing a major problem for the future king of Israel. Would I take the risk as did Abigail?

---

[1] The tearing of a robe or the hem of a robe was a highly symbolic act in the ancient Near East. First Samuel 15:27, 28 links the tearing off of the hem of a robe to the loss of the kingdom (see also 1 Kings 11:30-39). For further study, see Paul A. Kruger, "The Symbolic Significance of the Hem (*kanaf*) in 1 Samuel 15:27," in *Text and Context: Old Testament and Semitic Studies for F. C. Fensham*, ed. Walter T. Claassen, JSOTSup 48 (Sheffield, U.K.: JSOT Press, 1988), pp. 105-116; and Edward L. Greenstein, "'To Grasp the Hem' in Ugaritic Literature," *Vetus Testamentum* 32 (1982), pp. 217, 218.

[2] Robert P. Gordon, *I & II Samuel: A Commentary* (Grand Rapids, Mich.: Zondervan Publishing House, 1986), p. 179.

[3] David T. Tsumura, *The First Book of Samuel*, New International Commentary on the Old Testament (Grand Rapids, Mich.: Eerdmans, 2007), p. 581.

[4] The Hebrew text has here literally "son of worthlessness." ESV and NASB translate "worthless," while NJB has "brute" and the NKJV opts for "scoundrel."

[5] The following men took more than one wife and experienced numerous family problems: Abraham, Sarah and Hagar; Jacob, Leah and Rachel; Elkanah, Hannah and Peninnah.

Chapter 6

Uriah:
Faith of a Foreigner

Imagine...

Imagine a police reconstruction of Uriah the Hittite's last weeks of life:

Early spring: Under Commander Joab the Israelite army is deployed against the Ammonites, and they besiege Rabbah, which is 45 miles from Jerusalem. The siege lasts for weeks. The victim, Uriah, is deployed as part of a select military unit known for their loyalty and bravery. The prime suspect, King David, remains in Jerusalem and has a one-night stand with Bathsheba, the wife of the victim.

6 weeks later: Bathsheba sends a message via private courier informing the king that she is pregnant.

3 days later: The suspected coconspirator, Joab, summons the victim, Uriah, to headquarters and informs him that he is to go to King David to report on the military situation.

Assumed motive: In the absence of paternity testing, the prime suspect needs only to place Uriah at home for a brief amount of time in order to clear himself of paternity charges. There are no indications that the victim is aware of the encounter between King David and his wife.

4 days later: The victim leaves the military camp and travels 45 miles to Jerusalem. Uriah enters Jerusalem and goes straight to the palace, avoiding a slight detour that would take him past his home (his home is within sight of the palace). Uriah delivers his military report to the king. King David encourages him to take a few days leave at home. Uriah leaves the audience chamber and is seen in the servants' quarters of the palace. The king sends an expensive gift basket to Uriah's home with a thank-you note for his services.

Assumed motive: This gift was perhaps an attempt to placate the victim and help dissolve the situation if Uriah discovered that his wife was pregnant.

Following morning: A servant tells the king that Uriah did not return home but spent the night in the servants' quarters.

An hour later: The king summons Uriah and urges him to go home. The victim declines on the grounds that he is still on active military duty.

Early evening: The king invites the victim to dine and reportedly tries to get him drunk.

Assumed motive: If he is drunk, he will forget about being on duty and go home and spend the evening with his wife.

Third day in Jerusalem: Again, a servant tells the king that the victim did not return home but spent the night in the servants' quarters.

Same morning: The king sends Uriah back to the front with classified orders to Joab to see that the victim is placed in a dangerous situation and then abandoned to enemy fire.

Three days later: Uriah arrives in camp and delivers documents to Joab.

Following week: Uriah the Hittite is killed.

Meet the Cast

Uriah: In this story he is referred to as Uriah the Hittite. The Hittites of Palestine were an ethnic group who were somehow connected to the Neo-Hittite states to the north. Uriah was not the only Hittite to have served David. 1 Samuel 26:6 also mentions Ahimelech the Hittite. Uriah became one of David's elite warriors (2 Sam. 23:39; 1 Chron. 11:41). If Eliam, Bathsheba's father (2 Sam. 11:3), is the same person as is mentioned in 2 Samuel 23:34—Eliam, the son of Ahitophel the Gilonite—then Uriah married into a powerful Israelite family. His father-in-law would also have been an elite warrior and a son of David's esteemed counselor. This could explain the proximity of Uriah's house to the palace. Uriah's name is Hebrew and could be translated as "my light is the Lord" or "flame of the Lord." While he may have been a Hittite by birth, by choice he belonged to the God of Israel. Uriah's ethnic background underlines the fact that God does not look on the outside; instead, He knows the heart.

David: David is the main character in this story, as he is in many of the stories in this book. However, this story features a different side of David. We see none of the heroics of the battle with the giant Goliath. There are no glimpses of the shepherd, poet, or musician. This isn't even a love story. Here we see a man corrupted by power. The fact that this story is officially recorded in the biblical record is very unusual. It also serves as the pivotal change in the story and history of David. David had been going on from strength to strength, but now a downward trend begins. Even with true repentance, there are still consequences to bear that will affect the entire nation.

Bathsheba: In the biblical account, Bathsheba appears as a passive character, and the biblical author refrains from making any comments on her accountability or involvement. There seems nothing uncommon or provocative in her washing on the secluded roof of her home. The Hebrew verb used to describe David's "taking" of Bathsheba is very strong, suggesting that David's command could be translated as taken by force. The only time Bathsheba speaks is when she sends a message to David to say that she is pregnant (2 Sam. 11:5).

Joab: We meet again the seasoned general of David's army. By carrying out David's assassination orders, Joab becomes an accomplice in Uriah's murder.

Servants and messenger: Set in a time before a public postal system or direct communication via phone or e-mail, all communication takes place via people. These people are vital for the development of the plot. And, unlike electronic communication, people can read between the lines, and the rumors begin.

Background Information

War is ugly and seldom resolves issues. Most wars, once they are finished, carry in themselves the seed for a future war, since in most cases there is someone who feels thoroughly unhappy about the outcome. Scripture, unfortunately, contains many references to wars and battles. Some of them were ordained by God and involved the taking of the Promised Land during the settlement period. However, many of them were part and parcel of the human desire to become more powerful and more influential.

Did you know that God spoke to His people about principles of warfare? No, He is not condoning "holy war," a term that is never used in Scripture. The wars that were undertaken by God's people during the time of the Old Testament are "Yahweh's wars" and should not be confused with imperialistic dreams and desires of later kings of Israel and Judah.[1]

Deuteronomy 20 begins with the affirmation that Yahweh, the God who brought Israel out of Egypt, will be with His people—even when they face superior armies and more advanced war machines (Deut. 20:1). The chapter governs not only the calling up of the army (e.g., it requires those recently married or those who have recently established a vineyard to return home and not march in the army, as this would undermine their commitment to the land and to their family [Deut. 20:5-9]) but also the procedures to follow when the enemy city (or army) has been reached.

First, a peace offer is to be submitted (Deut 20:10-12). If that is rejected, the city is to be attacked and all men are to be executed. The legal system distinguishes between those cities that are within the borders of Canaan and those outside. Due to its idolatrous influences, all the inhabitants of the Canaanite cities taken during the settlement period were to be destroyed (verses 16-18).

There are also specific laws about siege warfare and procedures (verses 19, 20). For example, fruit trees are not to be cut down, as they can supply the Israelite army with food during the siege.

War is ugly and destructive. While God sanctioned some specific wars during the theocracy and theocratic monarchy of the Old Testament period, He did not give a rationale for later "holy wars." He should be recognized as the Divine Warrior whose support guaranteed Israel's continued existence but depended also on Israel's commitment. In the New Testament God makes Himself vulnerable when He comes to earth as a helpless peasant child. No bodyguards or Praetorian Guard. No divisions or legions guarding his arrival and ministry. His humble service conquered hearts and toppled kingdoms. And ultimately His sacrifice will win the victory in the great conflict between God and Satan.

Action

Although we are focusing on the character of Uriah, his story is embedded in the story of David. David's adulterous act begins and ends with a war against the Ammonites. The story begins in 2 Samuel 11 with David staying at home as the rest of his army, together with Uriah, marches toward Rabbath. While the Israelite army lays siege to the city, Satan lays siege to David's heart. Unlike the city, which holds out for more than a year, David capitulates immediately. The rest of chapter 11 details David's cover-up attempts, which at the end of the chapter appear to have been successful. David seems to have committed the perfect crime, but the parting line in the chapter brings in God's perspective on the drama that has been unfolding: "The thing David had done displeased the Lord" (2 Sam. 11:27, NIV).

Chapter 12 begins with Nathan the prophet telling a story, followed by the exposure of David's sins. It describes the first casualty of David's sin: the death of Bathsheba's child. However, the story is also about forgiveness, and another child is born. Finally, the story winds up with David returning to Jerusalem.

This is a high-action story. There is a war, an adulterous act, an 80- to

90-mile round trip for Uriah, Uriah's murder, the birth and death of a child, and the final conquest of the city. All of these intense happenings are briefly summarized or mentioned by the author in a line or two. Instead of focusing on the actual actions and describing them in detail, the author skillfully draws us (i.e., the readers) in by making use of a lot of personal interaction between the main characters.

Our story particularly focuses on the dialogue between David and Uriah. We, as the readers, know why David has sent for Uriah and why he is so eager to see him visit his wife. However, Uriah thinks that he is delivering a military report. The way the story is written is in some ways similar to the story of Job. In the opening chapter of Job readers are also taken behind the scenes and are allowed to witness some of the cosmic struggle between God and Satan. We then watch Job suffer and lose everything and wonder why everything is going so wrong. We don't have any insights into Uriah's thoughts on David's behavior—especially on the second day after Uriah has just demonstrated his loyalty to king and country by sleeping with the servants and is met with insulting accusations by David. And so, Uriah dies, loyal to the end. His story is an inspiring example of faith and loyalty without even the benefit of the big picture.

Digging Deep

Although Uriah is listed as one of David's mighty men (2 Sam. 23:39), it is only briefly in the darkest incident of King David's life that we get to know this background figure. Uriah, of course, comes into the story through his wife. It is interesting to note that after Bathsheba has been identified by name in 2 Samuel 11:3 she is simply referred to as the woman (verse 5) or later Uriah's wife. Although many people have speculated about her role in the story, the writer does not assign her any explicit blame. Remember, this was a culture in which women had limited rights. The way the writer stops using her name indicates that this was not a love relationship or an affair but rather a simple question of seeing, lusting, and wanting on David's part. The biblical narrator wants to emphasize that David has forgotten who he is and where he comes from. He now sees himself as any other king of the surrounding nations. When he wants something, he takes it. He sees himself as somehow being above God's law.

As soon as he realizes that his actions have consequences—Bathsheba is pregnant—David sends for Uriah on the pretext of obtaining battle news (2 Sam. 11:6). As the story progresses, we clearly see how David, who has been God's "model" king, slips lower and lower—he commits adultery, lies about the situation, attempts bribery, makes a good man drunk in order to make him break a vow, and finally orders his murder. Of course, David does not see the end results of his sin. He thinks that if he can get Uriah home for a short visit then his adulterous act will be camouflaged. Although some may argue that Uriah has heard some sort of gossip in the palace, the way the writer records Uriah's answers indicates that he has no idea of what has happened. In his meetings with David, he comes across as a man of direct honesty and unquestioning loyalty.

After receiving his battle report David sends Uriah home. The expression used in verse 8, to "wash your feet," may be an encouragement to make himself comfortable and by extension sleep with his wife or it may be a euphemism for sexual intercourse. In any case Uriah seems to understand exactly what David is implying, and he mentions it specifically in verse 11. In this case the king is by far exceeding his authority, and in either case he is encouraging Uriah to break God's law, which stated that soldiers were to be ceremonially clean when going to battle as God's presence was to go with them (Lev. 15:18; Deut. 23:9-11). Incidentally, this regulation also prevented war rape or abuse of female prisoners.

After Uriah leaves the palace David sends him a gift. It is interesting that the gift gets sent afterwards. Perhaps David had a feeling that Uriah would find a way to respectfully refuse the gift. In effect the gift is meant to force Uriah into a position in which he is obliged to follow the king's wishes. Uriah is not a man that can be bought. In the ancient world, gift-giving often implied some kind of obligation to the giver by the receiver.[2] Even with David sending him a gift to encourage him to go home, Uriah was not bought.

After being told that Uriah did not go home but remained in the confines of the palace, David sent for him again. His speech is anything but polite. King David is very insulting in verse 10. The situation is quickly slipping out of David's control. He is becoming frustrated. Uriah is showing him up. David's questions to Uriah are now personal attacks on Uriah's manliness. David, who was once a man of principle, now cannot understand Uriah's principles.

With Uriah's reply in verse 11 David realizes that here is a man whom he cannot flatter, bribe, or even command to break his principles. Uriah's argument is flawless. His answer shows that he is not a nominal believer, but he has completely identified himself with the God of Israel and his comrades. Uriah believes that it is wrong to use his situation for personal comfort or advantage. David, who himself was loyal to King Saul while he was persecuting him, cannot see past his current mess and does not understand the loyalty and faithfulness of Uriah.

Uriah begins his rebuttal to King David with the most visible form of God's presence: the ark. The ark sometimes accompanied Israel's army,[3] and although this was not the case in this particular battle, Uriah is convinced that God's presence was again with Israel's army. If God Himself was involved in the military action and all his comrades were roughing it in the open, what right did he have to have a vacation and unfit himself from taking part in the battle which was still to follow? Uriah ends the verse with a binding promise of solidarity to God and God's army.

In verses 12 and 13 we see David, in his desperation, resort to a disgusting scheme. He deliberately gets Uriah drunk in an attempt to break down his principles. It is interesting to note that the same scheme was used by the two daughters of Lot, which led to the origin of the Ammonites (Gen. 19:30-38)—the very people that the Israelite army is currently fighting. But despite his impaired reasoning, Uriah refuses to compromise his values, and he again spends the night among the king's servants. Just how costly this will be, Uriah has yet to learn. It is so ironic that David who as king fails to lead his men into battle ends up sleeping with another man's wife while Uriah, the foreigner, fights Israel's battles and refuses to take advantage of a situation to even sleep with his own wife.

David is desperate to find another solution, so he sends Joab a message with Uriah's death warrant. The cruel irony seems to be that Uriah is most likely to have carried the letter himself. Verse 17 states matter-of-factly that Joab carried out David's orders. Joab, of course, often showed disrespect for David's orders, but in this case he seems to have no qualms, even though it seems as if Uriah was one of his best men.

David was well versed with military strategy, which suggested that once a city was surrounded the besieging army simply had to have patience and wait for supplies to run out. Then, when the defending army was weak from sickness and disease, the besieging army would attack the city. The besieging army was normally careful not to get too close to the walls from which they could be targeted by the soldiers on the wall.

The messages that go back and forth between Joab and David in verses 18-27 give us a glimpse of the type of man David used to be and the depths of depravity to which sin had led him. David, who seemed to value his soldiers' lives, was never a reckless general, sending his troops on suicide missions. Perhaps David had not thought through the whole issue of having Uriah killed. If he had, he would have realized that it was near impossible to do away with him in a military exercise without his fellow soldiers becoming involved. Joab, who seems to have known exactly how to read David's directive, carefully instructs the messenger to appease David by adding the bit about Uriah. From the report in verse 23 it seems that the messenger is completely oblivious to the need to read David's mood and simply reports that Uriah as well as some other men have been killed. David's reaction is quite out of character. No regret is expressed, and the normally patient David even goes so far as to suggest that Joab step up the action that will in effect lead to more unnecessary deaths for the Israelite army.

Joab includes an interesting reference to the battle of Thebez in verse 21. While the story recorded in Judges 9 would have been well known and served as a warning about the dangers of getting too close to the wall, the reference to a woman killing Abimelech is interesting as it probably hints at the fact that Joab knows or at least guesses what is going on. While David is at pains to keep the scandal under wraps (and from the people), God knows the whole story, and He does not remain silent.

Issues

Being a foreigner: Foreigners did not have it easy in the ancient Near East in the time of David. Countries very seldom had embassies or consulates in other countries. As a foreigner one was alone and without official protection. Since blood ties, family, and tribes were so important in biblical times, someone without blood ties, family relations, and tribal loyalties found themself in an uncertain situation.

Foreigners in Israel were not exposed to arbitrary abuse or discrimination. Where there were definite legal prescriptions detailing the political, economic, or cultural "handicaps" of a foreigner,[4] there were also indications that foreigners could become part of Israel, in the fullest sense of the word. Just remember Ruth who became an important part of the Messianic line.

Foreigners could offer sacrifices (Lev. 17:7; 22:18) and participate in the three main festivals (Deut. 16:11, 14); however, they could not eat the Passover meal unless they had been circumcised (Ex. 12:43, 48). Foreigners were under the same legal restraints and obligations as were Israelites (Ex. 12:49; Lev. 24:22), a fact that is way ahead of its cultural and political time and due to God's specific intervention. After all, Israel needed to remember that they, too, had been foreigners in a strange country. They had been afflicted by oppression, and God instructed them never to afflict the same pain on foreigners living among them (Ex. 22:21; 23:9).

In our global economy with a significant number of people moving between cultures and countries, a foreigner most likely lives next door to you, shops at the same stores as you do, and sits in your pew in church. Have you ever stopped to think what life would be like if you were a foreigner living in a strange country, speaking a strange language, and missing your family and the familiar sounds and tastes of your own culture?

Re-action

Chantal: Sin isn't fair and is bigger and more insidious than I can imagine. In the story of Uriah, I'm struck by all the collateral damage of David's sin—Uriah, a good man, and several other men are killed in David's requested cover-up battle. Imagine all the wives that lost husbands and all the children who grew up without fathers. And then there is Bathsheba's newborn baby who dies. As part of the consequences for David's sins, during his reign he dealt with a rape, a murder, and a rebellion in which hundreds of people lost their lives. David's poor choices and poor fathering skills laid the groundwork for these problems. If only David had seen where it would all be leading to. I wonder how far-reaching and impacting my decisions will be on my children, husband, family, and friends. Sobering!

Gerald: Having lived for more than 20 years outside my own culture and home country, I admire Uriah the Hittite. He seems to have truly identified with his host culture. He was not only a committed soldier but also a faithful husband and a strong supporter of his king. Being a foreigner is not always easy. I may not know the language. I definitely do not (yet) understand the culture with its taboos and unwritten laws and mechanisms. I may not comprehend its most important values and may long for different expressions of love and community—just the way I know from back home. Am I ready to embrace a new culture with the same zeal as Uriah? Am I willing to be a home for somebody far away from home?

---

[1] A very helpful and readable introduction to war and warfare in the time of the Old Testament can be found in Michael G. Hasel, *Military Practice and Polemic: Israel's Laws of Warfare in Near Eastern Perspective* (Berrien Springs, Mich.: Andrews University Press, 2005).

[2] See, for example, the reply of the man of God from Judah in 1 Kings 13 who refused a gift from King Jeroboam and even refused to eat or drink with him or anywhere in the land of Israel by order of God.

[3] The ark accompanied the army into battle, as was the case in the battle of Jericho in

Joshua 6, in which a wonderful victory was won. Unfortunately, the ark was captured when Eli's wicked sons tried to force God into giving Israel a victory by bringing it into battle. 1 Samuel 4 documents Israel's defeat and the loss of the ark.

[4] No foreigner could become a king (Deut. 17:15). Similarly, debt was not automatically released after seven years for a foreigner, as was the legal intent of Deuteronomy 15:3. Many scholarly papers discuss whether this was ever a practice. The issue of debt and money reappears as a problematic item on the national agenda in Nehemiah 5. Foreigners could also not enter the sanctuary unless they were circumcised (Eze. 44:9). See Christopher T. Begg, "Foreigner," in *Anchor Bible Dictionary*, vol. 2, p. 829.

Chapter 7

Abiathar:
The Priest That Was, and Wasn't

Imagine...

Imagine the unemployed Abiathar looking for a job and writing a covering letter that he sends off with his résumé.

> Employment Recruitment Centre
> 3600 Main Road
> Jerusalem

Dear Sir,

If you have a client seeking an experienced advisor and strategist, I would like to make a strong case for myself. My counsel and advice in religious and political matters have helped to establish and enhance the royal house of King David. My political vision seems to have outgrown that of my former employer so the time seems right to move on.

It may be of interest to your client to know that I have closely served King David for more than 40 years. I demonstrate presence of mind during crisis situations as revealed by the fact that I saved the ephod during the massacre of the priests of Nob by former King Saul. I served as a confidant for King David when he was an outlaw hiding in the Judean desert. During my career I have also provided successful strategic military advice. I have demonstrated my leadership skills and organizational ability with the transfer of the tabernacle from Baalah of Judah to its current location in Jerusalem where, together with Zadok, I have been responsible for the organization and smooth running of the daily sanctuary service and the extra yearly feasts and celebrations. Due to my long associations with the founders of this dynasty, I also bring with me a wealth of political connections.

I would like to meet with you to discuss any employment opportunities that may be available at this time. I can be reached at my home in Jerusalem.

Sincerely,

Abiathar, son of Ahimelech

Meet the Cast

Abiathar: He is the only surviving son of Priest Ahimelech, a descendent of Eli. Abiathar fled the massacre of Nob that Saul ordered after suspecting that the priesthood of Nob was conspiring to collaborate with his rival David (1 Sam. 22:6-19). Abiathar rescued the ephod, the divine means of communicating God's will to the high priest, and brought it to David and his band of outlaws (1 Sam. 23:6). From this moment on Abiathar is part of David's team and a close confidant of the future king. During the succession struggle in the final days of David's reign, Abiathar joins Joab in support of Adonijah (1 Kings 1:5-7), while Zadok, belonging to a different priestly family, supports Solomon (verses 8-10).

David: David is, of course, one of the central figures in the books of 1 and 2 Samuel. His influence can be felt throughout the Old and even the New Testament. Abiathar's story is entwined with the story of David.

Zadok: Along with Abiathar, he was a priest for David. He remained loyal to David during Absalom's rebellion and collaborated with Hushai to pass on information to David (2 Sam. 17:15, 16). Later, working together with the prophet Nathan, he anointed Solomon as the future king of Israel, following David's orders (1 Kings 1:26-45). After the banishment of Abiathar, he assumes the main priestly functions.

Ahimelech: He was the father of Abiathar. Ahimelech was a priest during the time of Saul. Unaware that David was being hunted by Saul, he gives David holy bread and the sword that belonged to Goliath. Later, Saul massacres Ahimelech and his entire village for giving aid to David (1 Sam. 21).

Saul: He is the first king of Israel. By the time he enters our story, he is extremely neurotic and suspicious of everyone. He considers David his archenemy and spends his time and the country's resources in trying to track down and kill David.

Jonathan: He is the son of Abiathar who served as a messenger for David, carrying information from Hushai the spy after David and his supporters had fled the city during Absalom's takeover of Jerusalem. He, together with the son of Zadok, was hidden in a well by a woman (2 Sam. 17). Later he is the one to deliver the news of Solomon's coronation to the self-crowned Adonijah. He was most probably exiled to Anathoth with his father (1 Kings 2:26, 27).

Absalom: He is a very good-looking young man who is a scrupulous politician and strategist. Absalom murders his older brother Amnon who had raped his sister Tamar. With Amnon out of the way he is now in line for the throne. After setting out to win the hearts of the people, he rebells against his father David and declares himself king (2 Sam. 15). Only after a bloody battle, during which Joab kills him, is the kingdom restored to David.

Adonijah: He is David's fourth son, by his wife Haggith (2 Sam. 3:4). After the death of his older brothers, he positions himself to be king without David's knowledge or permission. Abiathar backs him in his attempt (1 Kings 1:7). After David abdicates in favor of Solomon, Adonijah again attempts to gain the throne through a passive request of marriage, but upon hearing his request, Solomon orders his execution (1 Kings 2:12-27).

Background Information

Priests and Levites played significant roles in the life of ancient Israel and were considered "personal attendants to Yahweh in His house."[1] Their primary function was the service at the tabernacle (or later the Temple)—even though they also had different roles. Priests were directly involved in the Temple rituals and sacrifices while the Levites functioned as the support staff in charge of carrying the ark of the covenant as well as the tabernacle elements when they had to be moved (Joshua 3:3, 8:33; 1 Sam. 6:15; 2 Sam. 15:24).

During the reform initiated by King Hezekiah, priests and Levites worked together to clean the Temple grounds (2 Chron. 29:6-16). Faced with lesser opportunities for service, once the Temple had been built, Levites became more specialized in their service for God. They functioned as gatekeepers (1 Chron. 9:18), security guards (2 Chron. 23:6, 7), bakers of the showbread (1 Chron. 9:31), Temple treasure supervisors (1 Chron. 26:20), choir directors and musicians (1 Chron. 9:33), and teachers of the oral and written law (Neh. 8:7-11).

Priests were generally not involved in the social life of the people, and unlike many of the prophets of Israel that decried social conditions (Amos 2:6-16; 5:11, 12; Micah 6:9-12), they kept a much lower public profile. During the struggle between Adonijah and Solomon, Zadok and Abiathar played key roles of support for the respective camps, as did the high priest Jehoiada during the reign of Athaliah when he saved young Joash and hid him in the Temple (2 Kings 11:1-17). However, these examples seem to be the exception rather than the rule.

Unlike the surrounding nations of the ancient Near East, priests in Israel, while closely interacting with the royal house, had much more independence and leeway than their counterparts in Egypt, Babylon, or Assyria. When King Uzziah of Judah becomes so enthralled by his own success story that he forgets his place in the larger context of God's plan and purpose and decides to enter the holy place and offer incense to the Lord—a task reserved for the priests—Azariah and 80 valiant priests keep him from entering the first apartment of the Temple and chastise the king (2 Chron. 26:17-19). The king, who has the power to sentence them to death, is not pleased with their courageous stand but is stricken with leprosy.

Another important aspect of priestly ministry involved blessing the community during feasts such as the Passover (2 Chron. 30:27). As is the case for most stories in Israel, priestly service begins with a genealogy to establish blood relations for the sacred office (1 Chron. 6:1-80; 9:10-34).

The ministry and function of the priests and Levites during the biblical period highlights an important principle: context influences and transforms roles without necessarily contradicting prior appointments. During the wanderings in the wilderness Levites were the prime "movers" of the tabernacle while the priests ministered in it once the tabernacle had been set up. After the construction of the Temple these roles changed (since Scripture reports few instances of the movement of holy furniture or utensils from the Temple) and led to an increased specialization in administration of the Temple and its worship. When the first Temple is destroyed, the priests and Levites need to refocus once again, and instruction appears to be one of the major outlets of their ministry during this time.

Action

Abiathar truly is a background figure. There are no particular chapters in which he steps onto the center stage. Abiathar's story spans a lifetime of service to David and his household. That is not to say that Abiathar led a passive or boring life. As David fled from Saul, he headed for Nob. This is Abiathar's childhood home, for the tent of the Lord was pitched there. David visited Nob and the priests for guidance during this dangerous and perplexing time of his life. Unfortunately, David was not honest with Ahimelech, Abiathar's father (1 Sam. 21:1-9). Upon hearing that David had been with Ahimelech, the insanely jealous King Saul had all the priests and their families killed, and he completely destroyed the town (1 Sam. 22:19, 20). Exactly where Abiathar was in all of this and why he wasn't with the other priests at the meeting with King Saul, we are not told. But we do know that Abiathar, who was probably a little younger than David, suddenly found himself a refugee. He fled to the wilderness and found David and his army (1 Sam. 22:20-23).

Abiathar joins David's band of refugees and travels with the group until David becomes king, first at Hebron and then as king over all of Israel. Later on, Abiathar tries to flee with David as Absalom's army invades the city, but David sends him back to be his undercover information courier (2 Sam. 15:24-29). In the end, his history as David's trusted adviser saves his life. Solomon graciously sends Abiathar back to his fields in Anathoth, even after Abiathar throws the weight of his influence behind David's son Adonijah rather than Solomon, whom God had chosen, in Adonijah's attempt to seize the throne (1 Kings 2:26).

Abiathar's life speaks of the power of example. We have no record of Abiathar's personal opinions, politics, or religious views. Everything he says is recorded as God's word to David, but his actions speak louder than words. Even though he is not recorded as saying anything, just being there makes a powerful statement.

As we examine Abiathar's life, we realize that we may not hold any important office or be especially talented at anything but we all possess the power to influence others. We see in the life of Abiathar how our personal influence can help or hinder God's plans.

Digging Deep

Almost since the beginning of the Christian church, theologians have had heated debates about predestination and freedom of choice. Based on a few biblical passages, such as Romans 8:28, 29, some people assume that God arbitrarily marks some people to be saved and others to be lost and that they have no free choice in the matter.

Contrarily, others have pointed out that many Bible texts stress the role of the individual's choice.[2] In order to find the harmony between the various biblical passages, we can look to the Old Testament. In the story of Abiathar, we find the practical outworking of both God's decision and Abiathar's freedom of choice.

Let's begin by looking at the background of Abiathar's dismissal from the priesthood. A quick reading of 1 Kings 2:27 may give the impression that Abiathor is dismissed because of a prophecy made to Eli years before Abiathar was even born. Solomon was not the oldest son and so by custom would not normally have succeeded his father as king. The oldest son, Amnon, had been killed by his brother Absalom. Absalom in turn was killed during his unsuccessful coup attempt. And now the fourth oldest son, Adonijah, feels that the throne is his right. Adonijah confers with two of the established power brokers of David's administration, Joab and Abiathar, and he receives their support (1 Kings 1:7).

Solomon was younger than Adonijah and had a scandalous family background. His mother was none other than Bathsheba, the former wife of Uriah the Hittite whom David sent to his certain death (and thus murdered) in order to hide his affair with Bathsheba. But notwithstanding this, Solomon is loved by God (2 Sam. 12:24) and is clearly chosen by God to be David's successor (1 Chron. 22:9, 10). In the face of this uncomfortable choice between Adonijah and Solomon, it seems that Abiathar cannot reconcile himself with the potential public scandal of crowning Solomon king, so he falls back on tradition as opposed to God's revealed will.

Tradition can be very comforting and comfortable as it saves us from taking responsibility to think things through in the light of God's revealed will. It is much easier and "safer" to just say "we've always done it like this." By this attitude Abiathar is implying that he has outgrown God's leading. He is no longer fit for the priesthood if he is unwilling to be led by God's Spirit.

Abiathar's life is spared by virtue of the fact that he had shared in David's hardships, but he and his son are dismissed from the priestly line, and Zadok the priest takes over.

What we have in Abiathar's dismissal is a demonstration of the way God's will and our choice fit together. God knows what choices we and our descendants will make, and so He is able to prophesy the future by saying who will eventually be saved. God knew that just as Eli's sons disqualified themselves from the priestly office by their behavior, their descendant, Abiathar, would also disqualify himself from the priestly office by being unwilling to accept God's choices.

Issues

A kingdom of priests: Mission and vision statements are becoming increasingly popular in the business world. In order for a company to achieve its goals, it has to understand who it is and what its goals are. Israel as a nation suffered throughout its history from an identity crisis, which in turn made them confused about *why* they were a nation. At times it seemed like their main goal was to become a nation like the other nations. This attitude led them to demand a king and made them willing to adopt the gods and pagan practices of the nations around them.

Eventually, after the destruction of the Temple and the subsequent exile (effectively ruling out Israel as an independent political unit), they finally understood that idolatry was a recipe for disaster. The survivors of the exile decided that the main goal was to remain separate and uncontaminated from the surrounding nations. This led them to form lots of rules to preserve their purity.

Israel also began to perceive itself as somehow superior to those around them. None of this was what God had in mind when He called Abraham and told him of His plan to establish a great nation. God had already stated what their purpose was to be. They were to be a nation of priests (Ex. 19:6). And from this nation of priests would come the great High Priest—Jesus—who would make atonement for the whole world (Heb. 2:17). What exactly did being a priest involve? In the story of Abiathar we gain a clearer understanding of some of the duties and functions of a priest.

As a priest, Abiathar was to live in God's presence. People came to him to find out what God's will was. In fact we cannot find an example in the Bible of Abiathar speaking his own words. Abiathar became so closely connected with God that his words are recorded by the narrator as being the words of God (1 Sam. 30:7, 8).

Abiathar also spoke to God on behalf of others and interceded for them. As David and his followers left Jerusalem ahead of Absalom's army, Abiathar and Zadok were there with the ark of God to intercede for their safety and survival (2 Sam. 15:24).

After David fled, Abiathar returned to the city that was soon occupied by Absalom, and he became David's ears and eyes in enemy territory (2 Sam. 15:27, 28). The story of how his son Jonathan and Ahimaaz, the son of Priest Zadok, embarked on a daring undercover mission to bring information to David makes for exciting spy and counterespionage reading (2 Sam. 17:15-22).

Today, we are called to a similar work. The New Testament clearly teaches that all of us are a part of the royal priesthood and are responsible for sharing Christ in our communities and societies (1 Peter 2:9). Although a priestly ministry may not be as exciting as Jonathan and Ahimaaz's undercover mission, our mission is just as essential. Ours, like ancient Israel, is no self-calling. Jesus said, "You did not choose me, but I chose you and appointed you to go and bear fruit—fruit that will last. Then the Father will give you whatever you ask in my name" (John 15:16, NIV).

We are called to convey God's Word to individuals and communities. We are also called to offer intercessory prayers for our families, communities, and those around us. This is why the Seventh-day Adventist Church was called into existence by God. We are to communicate God's end-time message to our world. This makes us different from others. Only in fulfilling our God-given purpose can we avoid the danger of assimilation with the world or the practices around us.

Living in God's presence as a nation of priests will also stop us from forming an exclusive bunker mentality and make us outreach-driven.

Re-action

Chantal: As I studied about Abiathar, I saw someone who had outgrown his need for God. As he fled the massacre of Saul or lived in caves in the wilderness, I am sure he felt a need for God. He realized that his very existence depended on God's protection. However, later as he had a secure job, status, and influence, God and His will seemed to fade into the background. I have a strong aversion to hard times or suffering, but I have noticed that these times do keep me dependent on God. I really want to keep my sense of how much I need God even in the good times of my life. I don't want to "outgrow" my usefulness to God and others by warped ideas of my own importance.

Gerald: I like traditions. As a family we have certain family traditions for opening the Sabbath on Friday night. Traditions are powerful means of establishing a fix-point and are particularly useful in moments of transition and change. Traditions help us to understand our roots and our own history. However, I get worried when all that happens in the church is based on tradition. Truth is not determined by referring to the fact that we have always done it like this. May tradition and history be cherished without becoming the golden calf of a church that cannot afford to live in the past but needs to face the future with creativity and zeal. The best is yet to come—and it is not going to be the traditional way.

---

[1] Gerald A. Klingbeil, "Priests and Levites," in *Dictionary of the Old Testament: Historical Books*, ed. Bill T. Arnold and H.G.M. Williamson (Downers Grove, Ill.: InterVarsity Press, 2005), p. 818.

[2] Some of the other references used to support the theory that God decides who will be saved or lost include 1 Corinthians 3:12-15 and Romans 9:9-16. Some of the verses that state that the determining factor is the individual's response to God's free invitation are Ezekiel 33:11 and John 3:18, 19.

Chapter 8

Joab:
David's Weak Strong Man

Imagine...

Imagine that you discovered the following letter:

To: His Royal Highness, the Honorable Absalom, son of David
From: Joab, son of Zeruiah, Commander of the Army
Re: Barley Field and Related Issues

Dear Sir,

It has been brought to my attention that my barley field, which is adjacent to yours here in the vicinity of Jerusalem, was deliberately set on fire by your servants yesterday. I believe that you are aware of this development. As you know, the barley was ripe and ready for harvest. The burning of my field has incurred a significant financial loss for me.

I realize that I have been unresponsive to your two invitations to a meeting, but I have been involved in other pressing engagements. I understand that you want to meet with me to discuss securing an audience with your father, King David. In my opinion such a meeting with your father would be immature and would not garner the favorable results you desire. However, in view of current developments, I will arrange an audience for you. I have the ear of the king and desire, as always, to be of service to you.

Let me please remind you that it was my motivation and zeal that brought you back to the area. I took it upon myself two years ago to persuade His Majesty to bring you back from your exile in Geshur. I planned the "woman of Tekoa" event, spent considerable time coaching her in her lines, and carried the financial expenses. My goal was to bring you back into the political limelight in Jerusalem. I realized, however, that negative public sentiment had not completely died down concerning your involvement in the death of your older brother, Amnon, and for this reason, I did not facilitate an immediate reconciliation with your father the king.

Due to my extensive political experience and influence over the military forces, I believe my services to be invaluable to Your Highness in your future political aspirations.

I trust that in future dealings you will value my support as highly as I value yours.

I remain faithfully yours,
Joab

Meet the Cast

Joab: Scripture describes Joab (whose name means "Yah[weh] is father") as King David's nephew. The name of his father is not mentioned in Scripture, but his mother's name, Zeruiah, appears 25 times (thus suggesting her importance and influence), and according to 1 Chronicles 2:16, we are told that she is David's sister. Joab, together with his brothers, Abishai and Asahel, played a key role in David's ascension to the throne and his later government. 1 Chronicles 11:6-8 describes Joab's valor when he "went up first" to attack the Jebusites who controlled Jerusalem before it became David's capital. Joab was a military genius. Unfortunately, he also displayed a violent streak, as is evident in his coldblooded assassination of Abner in 2 Samuel 3:27. Joab was loyal to the house of David even though he seemed to have other ideas about how to go about things when faced with moral decisions or dilemmas.

David: David's interactions with his loyal commander-in-chief often seemed to bring out the shadow side of his reign as God's chosen king. After being crowned king in Hebron a second time (this time by all Israel, see 2 Sam. 5:1-5), he immediately sets out to establish a new capital, realizing that favoring one tribe or one region over another would not strengthen his kingship but rather debilitate it and set it up for further dynastic struggles. Following the conquest of Jerusalem (verses 6-16), David's second key accomplishment as king over *all* of Israel is a major defeat of the Philistines who, upon hearing of David's ascension to the throne, go after the newly established king in full force (verse 17). David's final strategic action during this crucial period is the transfer of the ark of the covenant to his newly established capital in Jerusalem (2 Sam. 6). Joab featured prominently during the first two moves but is not mentioned when the ark was brought to Jerusalem.

Abishai: He was David's nephew and Joab's brother. Abishai also served as David's army chief and was recognized as a valiant warrior, renowned for his boldness and courage. He saves David's life in a skirmish with giant Philistines (2 Sam. 21:15-17) and seems to have led a crack troop of 30 warriors, David's "marines" (2 Sam. 23:18, 19). Abishai is a definite hardliner in David's government (2 Sam. 19:21), and together with his brothers he is described by David as his adversary (or *satan* in Hebrew) after Abishai suggests executing anybody who had opposed David during Absalom's rebellion (verse 22).

Asahel: Joab's youngest brother also belonged to the crack troop of David's group of "thirty" (2 Sam. 23:24) and commandeered the fourth division of David's army (1 Chron. 27:7). Apparently, Asahel was a fast runner (2 Sam. 2:18), and he pursued Saul's general, Abner, after the battle at Gibeon. After ignoring Abner's repeated requests not to engage him in combat, Abner kills Asahel in self-defense (verses 18-23). This death set the stage for Abner's later assassination by Joab, avenging his brother's death (2 Sam. 3:26-32).

Abner: Saul's seasoned general, Abner propped up the weak reign of Ishbosheth during the first years of David's reign over Judah in Hebron. After being accused by the Israelite king of sleeping with Rizpah, one of Saul's concubines, Abner decides to change sides and offers his services to David who gladly accepts him into his court. He is assassinated (without David's prior knowledge) by Joab because of Asahel's death. For more information about Abner, see the chapter on Rizpah.

Background Information

The united monarchy of David and Solomon during the tenth century B.C. has been targeted by critical scholars over the past decades and its historicity has been questioned repeatedly.[1] In some quarters David and Solomon's mere existence, never mind the historicity of the biblical description of their reigns, has been questioned, even though the discovery of the Tel Dan inscription in 1993 seems to have silenced the most ardent critics.[2]

As already noted, the capture of Jerusalem from its Jebusite inhabitants early in David's reign marked a crucial point in his reign. By selecting a central location that was currently not under Israel's control and making it the capital of the kingdom, David begins the long task of "nation-building."

The archaeology of Jerusalem is complex and convoluted since most of the interesting areas that would most likely produce significant finds (such as the Temple mount and its adjacent area) are out of bounds due to their religious connotations for three major world religions: Judaism, Christianity, and Islam. However, an increasing amount of Iron Age I and early Iron Age II material is being found in current research which should invalidate the claim of some scholars who suggest that Israel was just a small and insignificant hamlet or town during the early monarchy.[3] Furthermore, it needs to be noted that David is not described in the biblical record as having devoted too much time to monumental construction and building activities—he was too busy defending and extending the borders of his growing kingdom. His remarkable victories over the Philistine archenemy (2 Sam. 8:1) and the fact that he received tribute from the Moabites, Zobahites, and Arameans (verses 2-8) and was diplomatically interacting with the kingdom of Hamath and other kingdoms (verses 9, 10) suggests that David's "mini-empire" was indeed large when compared to the tribal mosaic of earlier periods. Even though it appears that David's kingdom was far-reaching, it should not be confused with the major empires of Egypt, Assyria, or Babylon.

Joab was one of the key power players in the nation–building process. His loyal support of David (based also on blood links) and his capable military genius gave David a powerful "weapon" in his drive for regional control.

Action

Joab is first mentioned by name in 2 Samuel 2:13 in connection with the battle between the forces of Judah and the forces of Israel at the pool of Gibeon. However, it is clear that he must have established his position under David prior to David's first coronation. His name is mentioned in connection with his brother Abishai in 1 Samuel 26:6 when David spares Saul's life for a second time. During the years as a refugee the spotlight is definitely on David and his military prowess, leaving little space for the people around him.

Joab steps onto the platform of biblical history during the conquest of Jerusalem (1 Chron. 11:6-8) when he is the first to crawl through the tunnel and enter the fortified city of Jerusalem, taking it for David. During the rebellion of Absalom he commands David's troops fighting their Israelite brothers, even though he had earlier invested a considerable amount of time and energy in getting Absalom reinstated in court (2 Sam. 14). Joab's counsel is often helpful to David (2 Sam. 12:26-28), and he pulls him back into reality when he is mourning the loss of Absalom. He also chides David for organizing a census of Israel (2 Sam. 24:3), even though David, as king, prevails and ignores Joab's advice.

Following Absalom's unsuccessful bid for power, David appoints Amasa as the commander-in-chief of his armies, in order to bring about reconciliation (2 Sam. 19:13). However, Joab is not surprisingly unhappy about this move, and he kills Amasa (2 Sam. 20:10) and without much ado makes himself again the leader of David's army (verse 23).

In the final years of David's reign, Joab throws his support to Adonijah, David's son with Haggith (1 Kings 1:7). Most likely Joab was not trying to overthrow David or considered this a rebellious act. After all, Adonijah was the next in line for the throne. Joab must have been unhappy that the traditional sequence of access to the throne was not being followed. However, this move was the last drop that made the glass overflow, and Joab did not survive the ascension of Solomon.

Digging Deep

We do not find many long speeches recorded in the Bible in connection with Joab. Instead, the biblical narrative records him as a man of few words and plenty of action. And many of his actions are blood-drenched. In this section we will look at the longest recorded speech of Joab. Strangely enough, it is spoken through someone else.

2 Samuel 14 begins with Joab's observation that David is missing Absalom. David's family life had become decidedly messy. After committing adultery with Bathsheba and having her husband killed, David seemed to have lost the moral respect of his family. Perhaps his own sense of shame, even following his repentance, held him back from disciplining his sons. When David's oldest son, Amnon, raped his half-sister Tamar, David, although very angry, did nothing (2 Sam. 13:21). Tamar happened to be Absalom's sister. After coolly waiting two years until publicity surrounding the event had died down, Absalom had Amnon killed at a family celebration. Absalom then fled to his mother's relatives in Geshur and lived there in exile for three years.

Here, the politically savvy Joab sees a golden opportunity to kill two birds with one stone. Joab can ingratiate himself with David and score some points with the next potential king of Israel. He shows a great deal of craftiness as he goes about his plan. First, he sends for a woman from Tekoa (2 Sam. 14:2). Since Tekoa was also the ancestral home of Joab, he most likely knew the woman personally. The biblical narrative records that she was known for her wisdom. Why Joab needed a wise woman is un-

clear. It is clear, however, that she could speak herself out of a difficult situation. Being involved in a plot to manipulate the king was a potentially
dangerous undertaking.

In verse 2 we find Joab micromanaging the whole thing. He tells the
woman what to wear and how to act. He dictates her speech to her. And
he makes sure he is present in order to supervise the smooth running of his
"production" (verse 21). Since the king was the supreme judge and was
supposed to judge especially difficult cases, the woman's story is carefully
constructed to be believable and tricky.

The story contained a number of moral and legal conundrums. In his
judgment call David is faced with a clash of duties, namely, the duty to
avenge a brother's death (Ex. 21:12) as well as the duty to secure survivors
for the widow and her deceased husband (Deut. 25:5-10). In 2 Samuel
14:8 David judges in favor of the son and states that the death will not be
avenged. Step one has been completed successfully, and now Joab, through
the wise woman, pushes the case further. The king's judgment brings up
an issue of guilt. Even though the son will be 'allowed to live what will
happen to his guilt?

Whether or not the king has the right to forgive the son is not mentioned even though verse 9 raises the issue, which is, of course, a big issue
for David. Can he as supreme judge forgive Absalom? What will people
say? So far David has simply rendered a judgment without personally involving himself. In this discussion of guilt, the woman is skillfully involving David.

Joab, who has been with David for so long, knows that David is a man
of his word and gets the woman to insist on David taking an oath in God's
name, knowing that David will not be able to extradite himself from such
a promise even when it becomes clear that the story is a farce. David's
promise in God's name will stand (verse 11).

The woman's question in verse 13 skillfully points out that the king
has just set a legal precedent for the handling of the case of Absalom. If her
son could be saved from the consequences of his murderous actions, then
why can't Absalom be pardoned too? Joab's use of the people in verse 13
shows very subtle tactics. Joab is implying that Absalom was the heir apparent and so belonged to the people. The people wanted their prince
back. David will not have to worry about public opinion, which is being
orchestrated by Joab.

Verse 14 is the key persuasive text in Joab's whole argument. Joab uses
the imagery of spilled water to show that we must all die. In other words,

we will all face God's judgment eventually. And now, with a brilliant insight into God's character, Joab states that rather than being out to get us for our sins God actively "devises ways so that a banished person may not remain estranged from him" (NIV).

In a strange way this text prefigures the famous description of God's irresistible love in John 3:16. It is here that we see the great paradox in Joab's life. His theology seems to be sound. In fact, it appears as if he had a better understanding of God than many of his contemporaries, but, yet, he never seemed to allow that knowledge into his everyday life and behavior. He never claimed God's mercy for himself. We know this because he never extended mercy to anyone else either. In verse 15 the pretense of the case of the woman is kept up, but David already seems to be suspecting something. Her appeal about being afraid seems ambiguous.

In verse 16 the story is left behind and an appeal is made directly for Absalom. The king has already given the verdict in the woman's case, and now it is pointed out that Absalom's case is even more deserving of the same verdict.

Although it may seem strange to address David as an "angel of God" in verse 17, the term *angel* could also be translated as *messenger* or *ambassador* and would fit with David's role as the one who is supposed to uphold God's law. Finally, all disguises are thrown off, and in verse 19 David asks the woman if Joab had anything to do with the situation. The woman affirms that Joab planned and narrated the whole event. Surprisingly, David turns to Joab and commands him to go and get Absalom. After all this talk of mercy and not letting the sinner remain an outcast, it is a pity that neither Joab nor Absalom seem to realize or appreciate it or let a merciful God work in their own lives. Due to Joab's interference, the stage is set for an awful rebellion that would lead to a civil war.

Issues

Politically correct religion: Long before the time of Joab people have been using religion for political ends. Joab's basic problem was one that we can easily relate to. He wanted to be in control. He was never willing to let God be God. It is interesting to note that Joab follows David's orders even when they violate God's commands but has no trouble disobeying the king's express orders when he stands to gain something.

Although Joab is seen as being totally loyal to David during the early part of his reign, over the course of his life it becomes apparent that the only person Joab is really loyal to is, you guessed it, himself.

For him everything, even religion, had a political end and could be used for self-promotion. Joab recognized Absalom's potential and wanted to ingratiate himself with the future king. However, in Absalom Joab would meet his match. Joab receives no thanks for his initiative in bringing Absalom home. Absalom simply wants to use him, and he quickly shows Joab that he can be as cunning and dangerous as Joab. Absalom even burns Joab's fields in order to force him to arrange a meeting with David (2 Sam. 14:28-33).

After murdering Amasa (2 Samuel 20:10) Joab's actions are justified by linking loyalty to David and God. The people know that David is God's anointed leader, and by being loyal to him they are showing loyalty to God. Because Joab has connected himself to David (even though the king has explicitly distanced himself from Joab), the people are bluffed into believing that unquestioning loyalty to Joab means in effect being loyal to God. This is no new manipulation tactic.

Since the beginning of time, the devil has enjoyed confusing the issues. And today, more than ever, it is easy to confuse the issues in a life that is full of "moral landmines." Some noble purpose is used to list our support for something morally wrong.

In the story of Joab, we see a man who definitely knows the facts and understands the concepts of his religion but keeps trying to use God to achieve his own goals. While he may have all the theological knowledge of God, God has no actual relevance in his life. Joab thinks that because David has always been unable to do anything about his misdemeanors, he can live as he pleases and escape the consequences. Joab forgets that God is not David. God cannot be fooled, even though retribution may not come immediately, in the end "a man reaps what he sows" (Gal. 6:7, NIV).

Re-action

Chantal: I grew up in a wonderful Adventist home. I cut my teeth on Bible stories. While I am no theologian, I think that my theology is pretty much intact. After studying Joab's story, I want to resist using my religion as a tool to get my own way. I especially want to resist the temptation to use Bible verses to force my children into doing what I want them to. I also want to be careful to not use our family's prayer time to voice my own take on other members' behaviors. After all, my Christian life is supposed to be about God using me and not me trying to use God to further my positions or ideas.

Gerald: I have mixed feelings about Joab and his ambiguous actions. He is a man of conviction who does not mince his words and is also prepared to stick out his neck, going so far as to challenge the king. He is loyal and sometimes headstrong, thinking that things will only work out *his* way. He has no problems bending the rules if the end justifies the means. Hey, just a minute. I see all these characteristics around me (and also in me). Joab would fit perfectly into the tough world of business executives of the twenty-first century. Can you imagine Joab following Jesus and listening to His Sermon on the Mount? I imagine that he would go crazy with Jesus' command to offer the other cheek. I wonder how the "Joab" spirit that surrounds me is affecting my values and choices.

---

[1] For a discussion of the historicity of the tenth century B.C., see Gary N. Knoppers, "The Vanishing Solomon: The Disappearance of the United Monarchy From Recent Histories of Ancient Israel," *Journal of Biblical Literature* vol. 116, number 1 (1997), pp. 19-44 or Kenneth A. Kitchen, *On the Reliability of the Old Testament* (Grand Rapids, Mich.: Eerdmans, 2003), pp. 81-158. On a more popular level, see Gerald A. Klingbeil, "Straight from the Mule's Mouth: How Studies About the Ancient Mule Confirm the Bible's Accuracy," *Adventist Review* (July 16, 2009), pp. 14-18.

[2] The Aramaic inscription found at Tel Dan in northern Israel dates to the ninth century B.C., but mentions, for the first time outside the Bible, the phrase "the house of David" in reference to the royal family. The original publication can be found in Avraham Biran and Joseph Naveh, "An Aramaic Stele Fragment from Tel Dan," *Israel Exploration Journal* vol. 43, Nos. 2, 3 (1993), pp. 81-98. Compare also Paul E. Dion, "The Tel Dan Stele and Its Historical Significance," in *Michael. Historical, Epigraphical and Biblical Studies in Honor of Prof. Michael Heltzer*, ed. Yitzhak Avishur and Robert Deutsch (Tel Aviv: Archaeological Center Publications, 1999), pp. 145-156.

[3] See the helpful summary of the debate up to 2002 in Provan, Long, and Longman, *A Biblical History of Israel*, pp. 228-230. For a more recent update, read Eilat Mazar, "The Solomonic Wall in Jerusalem," in *'I Will Speak the Riddles of Ancient Times': Archaeological and Historical Studies in Honor of Amihai Mazar on the Occasion of His Sixtieth Birthday*, ed. Aren M. Maeir and Pierre de Miroschedji; 2 vols. (Winona Lake, Ind.: Eisenbrauns, 2006), vol. 2, pp. 775-786

Chapter 9

Rizpah: King-maker and Nation-builder

Imagine...

Imagine, while on tour in the land of Israel, you stumble across an old rusty historical marker on a hill somewhere in the region of ancient Gibeah. The marker may read as follows:

"This marks the spot where Rizpah, daughter of Aiah, helped to bring about intertribal reconciliation in Israel during the reign of David, son of Jesse, by her selfless and faithful actions. After her two sons Armoni and Mephibosheth, together with five other sons of the former King Saul, were killed and their bodies exposed here, Rizpah, a now childless widow, camped by the bodies and protected her dead from desecration by birds and wild animals. The execution took place at the beginning of autumn and Rizpah continued her solo vigil for many weeks. Publicity of her brave solitary campaign challenged King David to reconsider the harsh realities of dynastic rivalries and work for reconciliation."

Meet the Cast

Rizpah: As a concubine Rizpah formed part of the household of Saul (2 Sam. 3:7). Her children with Saul were considered part of the royal household. Her name means "glowing coal." The mention of her father's name, Aiah, suggests that her family must have been important, even though we do not know too much more. When looking from the outside, it seems as if Rizpah is a mere status symbol for a powerful man. However, 2 Samuel 3:6-11 is not the final word on Rizpah. Her actions in the later story found in 2 Samuel 21:1-14 suggest that she is in control of her destiny and functions as an example of commitment and loyalty—a fact that is neither lost on King David nor on the biblical author telling the story.

Abner: He is Saul's general and the son of Ner. Abner is an imposing figure in Israelite politics for more than a generation. In line with general practice in eastern societies, which was duplicated by David, Abner seems to have been a relative of Saul (1 Sam. 14:50, 51). Family and clan loyalties went deep in ancient societies. He is Saul's army commander and bodyguard (1 Sam. 26:13-25), and following Saul's death on Mount Gilboa, Abner is instrumental in elevating Ishbosheth as successor to Saul's throne. During this short-lived interlude of Israelite history, the capital of Ishbosheth is located in Mahanaim on the other side of the Jordan (2 Sam. 2:8, 9). Abner dies at the hand of Joab when trying to negotiate a change of sides (2 Sam. 3:27).

Ishbosheth: In some Bible versions, his name is also presented as Ishbaal (New Jerusalem Bible), based on the slightly different name in 1 Chronicles 8:33 and 9:39. This was due to the fact that many names that included the element "Baal" were often reinterpreted in biblical names as a "shame," which is the English translation of Hebrew "Bosheth." Ishbosheth appears as a weak character in the story, and his reign, which lasted two years, is presented as a footnote to the rising star of David. Following the insult of Abner's alleged or real sexual intercourse with Rizpah, Ishbosheth is assassinated by two of his men after the death of Abner at the hands of Joab (2 Sam. 4:6).

David: David does not need much introduction; however, it is important to note that in this story he is more reactive than proactive. Recognizing the bloodguilt that Saul's actions had caused for Israel as a community, he agrees to the terms of the Gibeonites. He is proactive inasmuch as he asks God's assessment of the cause of the famine (2 Sam. 21:1). When he hears of the unselfish commitment of Rizpah to guard the honor of Saul's family, he recognizes the importance of honor and shame in the larger context of nation-building, and he finally finds an appropriate resting place for the remains of Saul's descendents, thus creating goodwill from the tribe of Benjamin and other clans who may have held loyalties to Saul's house.

Background Information

The transition from the period of the judges to the monarchy in Israel is complex and involves many changes, the most serious one involving religious and theological concepts. When the tribal leaders of Israel observe the less than stellar performances of the sons of Samuel as judges (1 Sam. 8:1-3), they pay a visit to Samuel's headquarters at Ramah and demand that he appoint a king. Can you imagine the paradigm shift that was initiated in that moment? It would be similar to the Congress and Senate of the United States demanding that King George of England become the head of state—though not in a representative fashion as in modern Great Britain—and absolute ruler of the United States.

Samuel is appalled (1 Sam. 8:6). God is the heavenly king (Num 23:21; 1 Sam. 12:12) and should not be replaced by a human being—even a human being appointed by God. Do you note the immense conceptual difference? Judges were appointed by God and generally did not establish dynasties. Their children somehow never made the cut[1] and now Israel demands to be "just like the others."

Archaeologically and historically speaking, the period covering the transition in the eleventh century B.C. is known as late Iron Age I/early Iron Age II.[2] This does not mean that people started using metals then (they had begun earlier) or that all the metals used were made of iron (actually bronze was still the most used metal), but rather it is a method of dividing up history that was established by archaeologists working in Europe and that was later adopted by historians and archaeologists working in the Near East.[3] Israel was at that time a village-based society where village, clan, and tribe were the key words.[4] Israel's request for a king (and thus the establishment of a monarchy) fits nicely into the larger historical developments of the regions. It was also during this period or slightly earlier that the neighboring tribal entities of Arameans, Moabites, Ammonites, or others moved toward a monarchy.

Village-based economies were generally self-sustaining and very little cross-border trade was conducted during this time. In fact, since no nations in the modern sense existed, borders were fluid and could vary. This situation seems to be reflected in the biblical books of Judges and 1 Samuel, particularly noting the interaction between the coastal Philistines and the different tribes of the Israelites. Most villages were not fortified. Instead of walled towns, more often than not houses were clustered around an open courtyard and were an integral part of the defensive system of the town. The four-room house was the most frequent style of construction, involving an open or covered courtyard where most of the household activities took place. Most of the animals stayed in the courtyard or one of its adjacent rooms during the night. Other rooms were used for storing food, keeping utensils, and sleeping.

Saul's ascension to kingship was not a smooth one. After his designation and anointing, which was done in secret by Samuel (1 Sam. 9:1–10:16), the new leader had to demonstrate his abilities. Saul shows his mettle in 1 Samuel 11 when he rescues Jabesh-Gilead from the hands of the Ammonites. After this event, his kingship is publicly confirmed (1 Sam. 11:14, 15).

A final word about concubines in the Bible. Often, the modern reader equates the term "concubine" with "slave" (or, even worse, "sex slave"). Generally, a concubine was a wife of lower status whose children, however, were considered part of the household of the husband and were rightful heirs. Concubines are often named as mothers in biblical genealogies (Gen. 22:23, 24; Judges 8:31; 1 Chron. 2:46, 48). When Absalom tried to usurp the throne from his father, David, he chooses to publicly sleep with his father's concubines (2 Sam. 16:21, 22)—thus indicating his apparent power and superiority.[5]

Action

Rizpah's story is carefully interwoven with the story of the early monarchy. She appears at two crucial crossroads in the life of David, the second king of Israel, and her unofficial title as "king-maker" and "nation-builder" is appropriate considering the importance of her involvement in the stories. However, Rizpah's story is also a quiet story that is not marked by action, but rather by being. She *is* Saul's concubine. She *is* a mother and member of a royal family whose star is rapidly sinking. She *is* a woman in a time and age when being a woman was not always easy. However, in spite of these challenges, Rizpah does not whine about her lot, but through her being and her actions she becomes proactive.

Scene 1 of the Rizpah narrative takes place somewhere in Transjordan, off the center of Israelite politics, on the other side of the Jordan. Ishbosheth, one of Saul's surviving sons, had been made king of Israel with the help of Abner, the erstwhile commander-in-chief of Saul. The "son of shame" (as his name means in English) was not a heavyweight in Saul's house. He must have felt insecure, and in turn he is paranoid and believes that everyone is trying to overthrow him. In 2 Samuel 3 he insults Abner by accusing him of sleeping with Rizpah, Saul's concubine, which, if true, could have been construed as an act of rebellion (verses 7, 8). Ishbosheth does not even mention Rizpah by name. In his question to Abner, he references her as "the concubine of my father"—a piece of royal real estate. His question unmasks his character as a power-hungry leader. Rizpah is not seen as a person with a name, feelings, and a history. She is not the mother of his half-brothers (2 Sam. 21:8); instead, she is a pawn in a royal gamble.

Abner's indignant response is of a similar nature. Again, Rizpah is just "this woman" (2 Sam. 3:8), but the response does not make it clear if Ishbosheth's accusation was indeed true. Ancient translators of the Hebrew text have similarly wondered, and in some cases, they included references as to the veracity of Ishbosheth's accusation.[6]

Ishbosheth's question opens a can of worms that cannot be closed again. Abner, hurt in his pride and feeling the lack of recognition, decides to join David's camp. Abner's departure undoubtedly leads to the disappearance of Ishbosheth's rickety fiefdom. He is finished—and so is Abner, even though he does not know it yet.

Scene 2 of Rizpah's story continues several decades after scene 1. David is now the king of a much larger Israel—albeit the fractures are beginning to show. Following his personal struggles involving Bathsheba and Uriah, David's house is threatened from within—the rebellion of his favorite son Absalom (2 Sam. 15)—and from the outside—a famine is holding the land in its iron fist (2 Sam. 21). David seeks divine guidance regarding the famine and is told that there is "bloodguilt" (ESV) on the house of Saul, due to their breach of the divine covenant with the Gibeonites (Joshua 9). David meets with the Gibeonites, and they request seven of Saul's male descendents, whom they plan to kill in payment for what Saul did to their city. Sparing the son of David's friend Jonathan, and thus maintaining his side of the covenantal promise made to Jonathan (1 Sam. 20:12-17, 42), David takes the two sons of Rizpah as well as five of the sons of Saul's daughter Merab.

Obviously, David is the absolute monarch and does not require any consultation or congressional vote. Now, Rizpah is not only a widow, but she also has no more sons. After the seven members of Saul's family are executed, the Gibeonites leave their bodies hanging in the open during the entire harvest season. As in many cultures, death in Israel required closure and a resting place for the deceased, preferably in an ancestral lot. For Saul and his family, however, there is no closure, that is, if Rizpah would have not been there. The biblical author describes her sitting day and night next to the corpses, protecting them from scavengers. Her quiet witness reaches David, who in turn acts in a way that furthers nation-building. David seems to recognize that new beginnings do not always require prompt and decisive action but may also involve forgiveness and closure—even for an enemy. It is interesting to note that the famine does not end after the death of Saul's seven descendents but rather when the remains of Saul and his descendents finally reach their ancestral resting place (2 Sam. 21:14). That is closure.

Digging Deep

Talk is cheap; action is worth its weight in gold. Have you noticed that

Rizpah never opens her mouth in the two places in Scripture where she appears? Quiet, seemingly passive, and definitely underrepresented and underrated, she, nevertheless, is able to change the fate of the dynasty and move a nation toward reconciliation and a new beginning.

How can this be? In a world that is inundated with voices, sounds, images, blogs, and media, where the one making the most noise is usually heard, it is surprising to read and "listen" to Rizpah's quiet story. The first member of the cast of 2 Samuel 21:1-14 to speak is David. Faced with the reality of a famine, he calls out to God, literally. The Hebrew text says that he "sought the face of the Lord" (verse 1), which is another way of saying that he needed to know God's will and guidance.[7]

God apparently answers and the bloodguilt of Saul's family to the Gibeonites is insinuated as the cause of the famine (even though we are not told exactly what transpired). David again speaks in verses 2 and 3 as he summons the crafty Gibeonites (see Joshua 9). The Gibeonites respond collectively and lay down two important principles. First, the bloodguilt cannot be paid by gold and silver, and second, due to their status in Israel (remember, they were not citizens, but servants), they do not have the right to execute others. In the next verses there is a ping-pong-like dialogue between David and the Gibeonites, which results in their demand that seven descendents of Saul's family need to be executed in order to make substitution.

Having received the divine diagnosis of the current famine, David moves forward with their request. Seven male members of Saul's family are rounded up, with the noted and important exception of Mephibosheth, Jonathan's son who enjoys David's covenant protection.[8] Seven members of Saul's family are publicly executed by the Gibeonites at the beginning of the barley harvest.

It is here that Rizpah appears—quietly and without words. We are told that two of her sons were among the executed members of Saul's household (verse 8). She does not talk; she acts. She stays when the shame is made public. She protects the corpses of the executed members of her family against desecration and destruction. She guards them for approximately six months. We cannot really understand the hardship of her six-month vigil.[9] There is no food delivery service; she has to fend for herself.

During her vigil Rizpah does not utter a word. Her manner is a stark contrast to the vocal and eloquent Abigail, whose discourse changes the heart of an angry warrior. But somebody speaks to King David. David is told about the loyalty and courage of a widow holding on to the last shred of her family honor—the bodies of her executed sons.

Moved by Rizpah's quiet but powerful witness, David acts and national reconciliation begins. The bodies of Saul, Jonathan, Saul's other sons, and the seven executed members of his larger family are finally moved to the ancestral resting place, the land of Kish, Saul's father. The rabbis tell us that the bones were moved in procession through the territories of Israel.[10] There is no biblical basis for this, but it could have happened as part of the national reconciliation. Something did happen, however, because following this act, the famine is broken. God "answered prayer in behalf of the land" (verse 14, NIV).

Talk is cheap, but action will cost us. It requires involvement and often sacrifice, and it should always have one important agenda point: listen to God when He speaks.

Issues

Bloodguilt: Human life was highly treasured in Old Testament law. The shedding of innocent blood was considered a case of homicide (Gen. 9:6; 37:22; Num. 35:33; Deut. 21:7), and there was no sacrifice to resolve this crime. The killing did not always have to be done by the perpetrator himself. Nathan recognizes David as the one who killed Uriah, even though he did not thrust the sword (2 Sam. 12:9). Similarly, the murder of Naboth by King Ahab is clearly recognized as such, and Elijah pronounces judgment upon the king (1 Kings 21:18-24).[11]

2 Samuel 21:1 does not specify when and where Saul annihilated the Gibeonites, who had—treacherously—made a treaty with Joshua that guaranteed their existence (Joshua 9). The fact that they were Amorites and settled in the territory of Benjamin would have motivated Saul even more. The story of the execution of the priests of Nob by Saul's henchmen (1 Sam. 22:16-19) provides further support for the probability and plausibility of the bloodguilt of Saul's house to the Gibeonites. However, covenants made in the name of the Lord were holy and recognized God as the maintainer and guarantor of the treaty.

The gravity of bloodguilt is illustrated by the fact that its effects—a famine in this case—hit Israel not under Saul or his descendents but rather under David, who represented a new dynasty as the Lord's anointed. Clearly, bloodguilt is serious business; it symbolically "stains" the character of individuals and peoples and requires blood to effect purification. This illogical fact (how can blood remove stains of blood?) brings us to the most "illogical" act in history: the death of Jesus, the innocent Lamb of God and Messiah who substituted His life for the human race. Christ's death on the cross—His willing acceptance of the guilt of our sins—is the only way to overcome the bloodguilt of sin that has soiled humanity. His sacrifice provides a way!

Re-action

Chantal: Rizpah's story is very challenging. Something in me really cringes at the way this woman is handled by everyone like a pawn. There are so many elements that are culturally so far removed from my way of thinking, such as the way she was handled as a woman and the whole bloodguilt issue. Being confronted with her story, I am once again reminded that there are very different worldviews than my own, and even biblical history cannot be neatly labeled and put in what I think is the appropriate box. However, there are things that I can perfectly identify with: a grieving mother's love and loyalty that shows itself in extreme conditions and sets off a positive chain reaction.

Gerald: Rizpah reminds me that change is not always wrought by powerful people but rather by people that allow God's power to work in and through them. Small people. Tall people. Old people. Young people. I wonder how much of Rizpah's attitude and commitment are in me. Am I willing to do the mop-up operations with no hope of recognition just because I believe it should be done? How much of a power-person have I become in the face of a power-hungry society? While Rizpah did not always have a choice, when she did, she made her choice and it truly counted for eternity.

---

[1] One wonders why most good judges or kings, despite their close walk with God, did not have children who followed in their footsteps. As examples, we think of Gideon's son Abimelech (Judges 9), Eli's offspring (1 Sam 2:12-17), and Samuel's descendents (1 Sam 8:1-3). And what about David's sons Absalom and Adonijah or Hezekiah's son Manasseh, who turned out to be one of Judah's worst kings (2 Kings 21)?

[2] A very helpful up-to-date history is Provan, Long, and Longman, *A Biblical History of Israel.*

[3] Many archaeologists have lamented the use of this nomenclature due to its inaccurate nature. Tel Aviv University professor Israel Finkelstein suggested to call the period between c. 1150-1000 B.C. "Proto-National States Period" since it is during this time that the fledgling national states of the ancient Near East appeared. However, while greeted with interest, his proposal did not receive the necessary support to change a scientific paradigm. Compare Israel Finkelstein, "Toward a New Periodization and Nomenclature of the Archaeology of the Southern Levant," in *The Study of the Ancient Near East in the Twenty-*

First Century: The William Foxwell Albright Centennial Conference, ed. Jerrold S. Cooper and Glenn M. Schwartz (Winona Lake, Ind.: Eisenbrauns, 1996), pp. 103-123.

⁴ A very helpful summary of the history of Israel during the twelfth and eleventh centuries B.C. can be found in Robert D. Miller II, *Chieftains of the Highland Clans: A History of Israel in the 12th and 11th Centuries B.C.* (Grand Rapids, Mich.: Eerdmans, 2005), esp. pp. 97-103.

⁵ A concise discussion of the biblical data can be found in Mary E. Shields, "Concubine," in *The New Interpreter's Dictionary of the Bible*, ed. Katherine Doob Sakenfeld, 5 vols. (Nashville, Tenn.: Abingdon Press, 2006), vol. 1, pp. 713, 714.

⁶ The Lucianic version of the Greek translation of the Old Testament includes some additional notes in verse 7: "And Abner took her," following the name and house of Rizpah. However, since this is the only reference, it seems that it represents a scribal insertion, trying to make sense of an ambiguous text. Cf. Gordon, *I & II Samuel: A Commentary*, p. 217 (and note 31 referenced there).

⁷ The verb "to seek" is often used to introduce the main action in Hebrew usage. For example, Pharaoh "seeks" to kill Moses (Ex. 2:15), while in Exodus 4:24 it is God who "seeks" to kill Moses. First Kings 11:40 notes that Solomon "seeks" to kill Jeroboam. In this instance the focus is upon God's face, i.e., His guidance and spoken response.

⁸ It is important to recognize that while Saul apparently did not honor the covenant that had been established during the settlement period (in the name of the Lord), David does honor his covenant with Jonathan and his descendents—even those that are physically disabled, a curse in a society that considered a handicap to be a direct sign of God's displeasure.

⁹ See the helpful comments in R. G. Branch, "Rizpah: Activist in Nation-Building. An Analysis of 2 Samuel 21:1-14," *Journal for Semitics*, vol. 14, no. 1 (2005), pp. 82-84.

¹⁰ *Ibid.*, p. 84.

¹¹ A helpful introduction to the issue of bloodguilt can be found in Dale Patrick, "Bloodguilt," in *The New Interpreter's Dictionary of the Bible*, vol. 1, pp. 481, 482.

Chapter 10

The Nameless Prophet: Obedience Is Not Optional

Imagine...

Imagine this news headline:

Furor at the Dedication Ceremony
by our correspondent on the scene

What was meant to be the climax of the official dedication of the new shrine at Bethel by His Majesty King Jeroboam faded into the background in the ensuing series of dramatic events. At this morning's ceremony, as King Jeroboam stood before the altar making a sacrifice, a man identified only as *a man of God from Judah* began shouting. A court official, who did not wish to be named, says that he addressed the altar and said that someone named Josiah from the house of David would desecrate the altar. He also announced that the altar would be split apart and the ashes spilt out.

Understandably, this interruption to the program was not appreciated by the hundreds of dignitaries and attendees. The king publicly issued an order of arrest, but before it could be executed, the king's arm, which he was pointing at the prophet from Judah, shriveled up. A member of the king's security detail stated that "it was unbelievable. Before my eyes the king's right hand and arm shriveled up. We were all shocked. The king was just staring at his arm. I don't think he could believe what was happening."

To add to the confusion, the new altar then cracked open and the ashes poured out on the flooring. Apparently, after witnessing these events, King Jeroboam requested that the prophet from Judah intercede for him. Following the prayer of the nameless prophet, witnesses claim that the king's arm appeared to be normal. The prophet publicly refused the king's offer of lunch with royalty, stating that God had commanded him not to

91

eat in Israel, although several residents of Bethel claim to have seen the prophet accept a dinner invitation to the home of an older Bethel resident.

Late this afternoon travelers reported a body lying by the main road from Bethel to Judah. The body has been identified as that of the man of God from Judah. He appears to have been the victim of a very rare lion attack. Those first on the scene reported seeing a lion supposedly "guarding" the body while his donkey grazed peacefully nearby. Investigations continue.

Meet the Cast

Man of God from Judah: Although one of the central characters of this story, we are not given any personal information about this man. We only know that he comes from Judah. His title, "man of God," was a common phrase used for a person recognized as a messenger from God in the Old Testament. The title was used for Moses (Deut. 33:1) and Elijah (1 Kings 17:18). His title shows that he was associated with the "great" prophets—sadly, he failed.

Jeroboam: In contrast to the other characters of the story, we are given fairly comprehensive background information about Jeroboam. He was the son of Nebat and belonged to the tribe of Ephraim (1 Kings 11:26). We also know the town in which he was born: Zeredah. His mother was a widow. He became the first king of Israel after the united kingdom of Israel split into two kingdoms (verses 26-40) and reigned for approximately 22 years, beginning around 930 B.C. He was placed on the throne by the 10 tribes of Israel after the inexperienced (and seemingly headstrong) son of Solomon, Rehoboam, refused to lighten the heavy taxes. As a result, Rehoboam was left with the kingdom of Judah (1 Kings 12:20). Under King Solomon Jeroboam received administrative training and was promoted to a leadership position that supervised government work forces (1 Kings 11:28). He observed firsthand Solomon's glorious reign as he trusted in God. And he would also see how the consequences of idolatry ate away at the kingdom.

Like David, Jeroboam was called by God to be king (verses 30-39). Like David, Jeroboam was forced to flee and lived in exile in Egypt until Solomon's death. However, unlike David, Jeroboam never put his trust completely in God, and he was inclined to play politics to establish and keep his kingdom. It was political caution that led him to build and dedicate the shrines in order to keep the Israelites from going to Jerusalem to worship God (1 Kings 12:26-29). Because of the significant role that

Jeroboam played in leading the majority of the nation into idolatry, God promised to take the kingdom from his family line. In fulfillment of this prophecy, his evil son Nadab reigned only two years and was then assassinated, and his entire family line was wiped out (1 Kings 15:27-30).

Old prophet: Although he lived and was buried in Bethel, he seems to have originally come from Samaria. He was not present at the dedication ceremony and only hears about it from his sons. Why he follows the man of God and then lies to him, we are not told. He appears to be sorry for his deception because he sends the man of God off on his own donkey. Later, after the attack, he collects the body and buries it in his own grave. Strangely, he seems to be the only one who learns anything about God and accepts the word of God. He demonstrates his faith in God by asking to be buried with the man of God. This act saves his bones from being disturbed (2 Kings 23:18).

Sons of the prophet: They serve as witnesses, messengers, and background workers in this story. They represent the wider community's involvement.

Josiah: He is one of only a few people mentioned by name in prophecy prior to their birth. He was born about three centuries later and was the last good king of Judah. By this time the kingdom of Israel had already been wiped out by the Assyrians. He did break down the altar in the last great reformation (2 Kings 23:16).

Background Information

In order to understand the full implications of the story of Jeroboam, we need to examine it against the big political picture. Under King Solomon the kingdom stretched as far as Egypt in the south and the Euphrates river in the north (1 Kings 4:21, 24) and reached unprecedented heights of power and wealth. Solomon's marble and gold Temple became an architectural wonder. Israel was no longer a group of unknown tribes but had become a political power to be reckoned with.[1] All this growth, unfortunately, came with a price. Instead of realizing and acknowledging the blessings of God, Solomon, who had been handpicked by God and had been given wisdom and wealth, became self-secure and self-sufficient and gradually lost his hold on God. By marrying many foreign wives he opened the door for Satan's influence. Gradually, he not only tolerated the idol worship of his wives but he supported it by building places of worship for them and attending their worship services. This led to widespread idolatry within the kingdom of Israel. Israel, which had been chosen by God to be a living model of what every nation could be if they chose God as their god, was rapidly losing its divine purpose.

It was time for a wake-up call. For Solomon it was the message that this beautiful kingdom would be torn from him (1 Kings 11). For Solomon the wake-up call was not too late. He desperately tried to undo the harm done. During his wayward years, there were people in his kingdom who stayed true to God, but a large portion of the population had slavishly followed the religious fashions of the nations around Israel that the wise king had tolerated and even supported. But even a penitent Solomon was not able to reverse the downward trend that the nation had taken.[2]

After Solomon's death his son Rehoboam claimed the throne. Although Solomon had tried to give his son intensive training courses in kingship after his own reconversion, it proved very difficult to counteract the negative influence of his idol-worshipping mother and the fact that Solomon had let the formative years of the boy's childhood and teens go by without positive training or a good role model. All Israel assembled at Shechem where Rehoboam expected to be formally crowned as king. However, he did not seem to know his people at all. During Solomon's reign the king had kept a very large court, not to mention a large harem and his many ambitious building projects.[3] All of these projects were funded by taxes. A delegation at the coronation ceremony approached Rehoboam about reducing the tax load. Rehoboam showed definite despotic tendencies in his answer and narrowly escaped mob action. His minister of labor was not so lucky and was stoned (1 Kings 12:18).

After this encounter with Rehoboam, Jeroboam was placed on the throne by the 10 northern tribes of Israel (excluding Judah). This was not his lucky break. This outcome had been foretold by the prophet Ahijah the Shilonite many years before (verse 15).

Unfortunately, Jeroboam never felt secure in God's promise. He was worried about the Israelites visiting the Temple in Jerusalem, which was still under Rehoboam's control. Jeroboam concerned himself with possibilities, wondering if Rehoboam could win the popular vote again in the future. Instead of trusting God, the one who had given him the throne, Jeroboam turned to political scheming. If the Israelites could be kept away from the center of worship, then they would remain firmly under his control. And so he created, within his borders, two centers of worship: one at Bethel and the other at Dan (verse 29). In an effort to be more relevant, he decided to put something visible in the shrines that could represent God to the people. Ironically, he chose golden calves, which had brought the people so much trouble in their early history (verse 28). Idolatry and the worship of God were being mixed in a new, strange, and dangerous syncretistic form of worship in which basically anything went. Into this complex political and spiritual environment, God chose to reveal Himself in a spectacular way.

Action

In this narrative we see, in miniature, the great cosmic struggle between God and Satan played out in the decisions and actions of humans. This is no simple story quietly being played out in some humble home. Although there are only a few human actors, the story plays out on a very visible stage with hundreds of witnesses. At the beginning of the story, it seems fairly easy to label the different characters: King Jeroboam is obviously *against* God—he is dedicating a shrine with an image of a golden calf—while the man of God must be *on* God's side. However, when the lying prophet, who is also uttering prophecies, enters the scene, things get complicated. In all the action and counteraction we see the characters taking sides and changing sides—similar to the great controversy.

The story begins with King Jeroboam's action, which evokes a counteraction by God. A lot of geographic movement takes place in this battle for the heart of a nation as well as individuals. King Jeroboam goes to Bethel for the dedication ceremony. The prophet of God goes to Bethel. At Bethel there is a showdown. A prophecy is made that in part is immediately fulfilled. (The other part will only be fulfilled centuries later.) The king's hand withers and is restored. And then the prophet, after executing God's action, refuses the king's offer and claims that he will not stop in Israel to even eat or drink but will immediately go back to Judah as God commanded.

The sons of the old prophet leave the site of the dedication and tell their father what happened. The old prophet decides to chase after the man of God. Given the action-packed nature of the narrative, we would expect to find the man of God from Judah hurrying to the nearest town in Judah. But the story suddenly grinds to a halt as the old prophet finds the man of God calmly sitting under a tree.

After a brief exchange (in which we, as the readers, are horrified to hear how easily the man of God is taken in), the two men travel to the old prophet's home at Bethel. They eat and drink, and then God's word comes to the old prophet. The story reports no reaction from the man of God. Instead, the old prophet seems to be making active decisions and tries to undo some of the damage he has done by sending the man of God on his donkey. The story then focuses on the last strange act as the lion that kills the man of God is seen standing guard near the body while the donkey grazes nearby. In closing, there is the unlikely faith declaration by the old prophet as he buries the man from Judah.

Digging Deep

Experts tell us that well over half of our communication consists not in the words we say but in our body language. Body language includes the tone we use, our facial expressions, eye contact, what we are doing with our hands, arms, and feet, as well as the way our bodies are positioned. In a written account we have only the spoken words and a description of the action. This means that when the biblical account mentions body language in a story it has been done deliberately in order to call our attention to something specific. The story of the man from Judah contains several body language references. In this section we will look at three of them.

Let's begin with the king stretching out his hand in 1 Kings 13:4. The man of God has just pronounced a prophecy against the altar that the king is busy inaugurating. In effect he is pronouncing God's judgment on this whole worship system that Jeroboam has thought up. The text mentions that the king turns around and does not only shout for the man to be arrested but stretches out his hand. In the Old Testament, stretching out the hand always had to do with a show of power. Throughout the Exodus account God commands Moses and Aaron to stretch out their hands in the dramatic showdown with Pharaoh (Ex. 3–14). Every time a hand is stretched out something miraculous happens.

In Job 1:11 we have another dramatic showdown involving stretched-out hands. Satan challenges God to stretch out His hand against faithful Job. Satan wants God's outstretched hand to bring destruction to Job and everything he has. God does not stretch out His hand against Job; He does, however, give Satan permission to try to prove that Job loves God only for the blessings God gives.

In the prophecies of Jeremiah, Ezekiel, and Zephaniah it is predicted that God will stretch out his hand in judgment against various kingdoms (Jer. 51:25; Eze. 6:14; Zeph. 1:4). In looking a little at the background of this expression we can see several things emerging. First, stretching out the hand is mostly associated with God. Second, it often involves judgment. Now perhaps we can understand some of the dramatics involved in King Jeroboam's outstretched hand. He was instituting his own system of worship in direct defiance to God's instructions. As if that were not enough, he had the audacity to judge God's messenger and, in effect, God Himself by stretching out his hand. No wonder it shriveled up! This of course makes the second part of the story even more wonderful. Jeroboam immediately asks the man of God to intercede on his behalf. In His greatness and mercy God willingly forgives Jeroboam's rebellion as he hears the prayer of the prophet, and He restores the king's arm (1 Kings 13:6).

After this dramatic turn of events, the biblical author mentions that the man of God is found sitting under a tree (1 Kings 13:14). After stressing how important and urgent it is for him not to eat or drink anything in Israel and to return home, it is strange to find this man sitting under a tree. Even in modern times sitting is associated with waiting or relaxing, not with urgent activity.

Three times we find people sitting under a tree in the Old Testament. Mostly, they appear with positive connotations. In a beautiful love poem in Song of Solomon the lovers are described as sitting under an apple tree (2:3). In Zechariah 3:10 and Micah 4:4 the prophets tell of a future idyllic world in which everyone will sit under his own vine and fig tree. The state of the kingdom of Israel is far from idyllic with judgment having just been pronounced—and yet, the man of God is sitting under a tree. This detail tells us that he is setting himself up for a trap. The author of Psalm 1:1 nicely describes the smooth transition into temptation with someone *walking*, then *standing*, and finally *sitting* in sin. The detail of the man of God sitting under a tree speaks volumes about his lack of seriousness.

The man of God from Judah meets his end on the way home after the forbidden meal: a lion meets him on the road and kills him (1 Kings 13:24). His body is thrown down from the donkey, and then the readers are told twice that the donkey and lion stood by the body. Again, the details of the position of the body and the other two animals are meant to tell us something. This was no ordinary lion attack.

The fact that the man was attacked on a busy road is in itself unusual, but the fact that the lion did not eat or further maul the body but simply stayed near it is abnormal. The other abnormality is the position of the donkey. The donkey is not injured or traumatized, neither does it run back home. The animals and the body provide postmortem evidence that this is divine fulfillment of prophecy and was meant to serve as a very vivid reminder to all of Israel that God meant what he said.

97

Issues

In this narrative we have at least two men claiming to speak for God. In effect, they are claiming to be God's prophets. This was not a strange claim, as prophets and prophetic messages were widely recognized throughout the ancient Near East, even in the idolatrous countries surrounding Israel.

The Hebrew word *nabi'* (or prophet) refers to someone whom God calls to speak for Him. A prophet, called by God to deliver a message, was specifically responsible to God and was not employed by someone else. By their special calling the messenger was to demonstrate absolute loyalty to God. Their loyalty to God enabled prophets throughout the time of the monarchy to fearlessly point out the sins of the kings and people of Judah and Israel. This made God's prophets different from prophets in other countries where they were mostly employed by the king and obligated to "fabricate" positive prophecies that supported whatever the king had in mind.[4]

For God's messengers the gift of prophecy was really that—a gift. The fact that God chooses and uses someone to be His messenger in a particular circumstance does not mean that the prophet is above fault or has lost his freedom to choose for or against God. In Scripture Moses is considered as *the* prototype of a prophet. Before he died he told the Israelites that "the Lord your God will raise up for you a prophet like me from among your own brothers. You must listen to him" (Deut. 18:15, NIV). This prophecy was ultimately fulfilled in Jesus, who would lead His people—us—from the slavery of sin to our heavenly Canaan.

However, even Moses was disobedient at times. For example, he struck the rock instead of speaking to it as God had told him to do (Num. 20:8-12). When a prophet is representing God, there is a lot at stake. God's message must be given clearly and without distortion by the messenger. For that act of disobedience Moses could not enter the Promised Land. God, however, had something even better for His repentant messenger. Moses was the first to be raised from the dead and taken to the heavenly Canaan (Matt. 17:3). The Bible records another example of someone given the gift of prophecy by God who, instead of using his gift to serve God, seemed to be much more interested in lining his own pockets than representing God. It is tragic that the donkey that Balaam was riding proved to be a better messenger for God than the prophet himself (Num. 22).

In our story of the man of God from Judah we catch glimpses of the very human side to prophets. The man of God from Judah distorts God's message by sitting under a tree, and he follows what someone else says that is in direct contrast to what God has said. In the end we have a lying old man who is used by God and delivers the message and then believes the word of the Lord.

Re-action

Chantal: I often want to see more spectacular miracles in my life. I am tempted to think that this would make obeying God and witnessing for Him much easier. In this story of withered arms, cracked altars, and detailed prophetic forecasts I realize that this theory does not work. Sensational happenings are quickly forgotten or explained away and can never make up for simple faith in what God has said.

Gerald: Obedience has become a four-letter word. The media suggests that we need to be free, without any limits and restrictions, doing what we want to do—and doing it right now! The story of the nameless prophet reminds me about the importance of obedience according to God's perspective. This is not just an optional desideratum but is essential for surviving the greatest conflict this planet has ever faced. How much weight does a "thus says the Lord" carry for you?

---

[1] See Provan, Long, and Longman, "Solomon and His World," in *A Biblical History of Israel,* pp. 251-254. 1 Kings 4:34 and 1 Kings 10 give us a glimpse of the important international role that Solomon played during the middle of the tenth century B.C.

[2] Perhaps one of the most important legacies the wisest man on earth left us was a demonstration of the negative power of influence.

[3] Solomon built a new luxury palace for himself as well as for Pharaoh's daughter, which was one of his first foreign wives. For a description of his building activities, including the Temple, read 1 Kings 6 and 7.

[4] King Ahab seemed to have had a number of professional prophets in his employ, following the custom of the neighboring countries. They, of course, prophesied victory for the king's proposed war plans (1 Kings 22).

Chapter 11

The Widow of Zarephath:
The Leap of Faith

Imagine...

Imagine a brief thank-you note written by the widow to the prophet Elijah.

Dear Prophet Elijah,

What a blessing you have been to this home! We are extremely sad to see you leave. It seems like just yesterday that my boy and I met you as we were gathering some brush to cook what we thought would be our last meal. I will never forget the struggle inside me as you asked for bread—our last bread. I am so glad that I decided to give it to you. It was the very best investment I could ever have made. Although it happened every day, it was still just so amazing; there was enough flour and oil for the day's baking. For three years we experienced daily miracles. I, not even being an Israelite, stood amazed at the God of Israel's miracle-working presence in my home.

You always seemed so contented and confident living with God. I guess that comes from having done so much together with God as His messenger. For me it was a whole new experience having God's presence in my home. Day by day as you spoke of your God and worshiped Him, I became acutely aware of things in my own life. I began to see it in comparison to this great holy God. I became more and more ashamed. I think it must all have come to a head with the death of my son. As I sat beside his mat and tried to cool the raging fever, I seemed to remember every instance I had been impatient with the lad—the time I had scolded him until tears ran down his little face for knocking over the water pot, even though it was an accident. I remembered my husband and the last argument that we had. I came face to face with my selfishness. I wanted to ask God for help to heal my son, but I felt so wicked. Even my son's death could not be sufficient payment for my sins before such a holy God. Thank you so much for your gentle patience as I screamed at you after my son's death. And how can I ever thank you for giving him back to me alive! My boy lives, and now, every time I look at him I know that God has seen me with my faults and still hears and forgives me.

Thank you so much for showing me the living God!
The widow of Zarephath

Meet the Cast

Widow of Zarephath: She is an anonymous widow from the Phoenician town of Zarephath, near Tyre and Sidon. During the famine affecting Palestine in the time of the prophet Elijah she is in a desperate situation and faces starvation (1 Kings 17:12). Elijah finds refuge in her home after his departure from the brook of Cherith. Later, her only son dies and is miraculously restored to life by the prophet.

Son of the widow of Zarephath: He is a passive member of the cast and is only mentioned once prior to his death (verse 12). During the time that Elijah stays with the widow's family her son grows ill and finally breathes his last. Elijah's response and action in verses 19 and 23 could suggest that the son is younger and, thus, can still be carried easily by an adult.

Elijah: The prophet of Yahweh, he is living in the region of Gilead in the northern kingdom of Israel. His ministry affected the life of the house of Omri, the dynasty that established Samaria as the capital of northern Israel during the ninth century B.C. Elijah's main concern is for the sovereignty of God in the midst of a world that was slowly, but surely, moving away from the true worship of Yahweh and replacing Him with Baal or other deities of the Semitic pantheon. Because of the crucial mission of establishing the true credentials of sovereign Yahweh, Elijah is commanded by the Lord to announce a drought and subsequent famine, which is the result of the lack of rain. God hits Baal, the weather god of ancient Canaan, where it hurts. Elijah's name, "The Lord is my God," is part of God's plan. His name not only has a nice sound to it in Hebrew, but it points to the conviction of God's lordship over the life of His people—and creation as a whole. Elijah's most momentous moment in life occurs on Mount Carmel during the important encounter between Yahweh and Baal—represented by the scores of the prophets of Baal, and Elijah.

Background Information

Geography plays a major role in this story. Elijah leaves the confines of the territory of Israel after surviving miraculously near the wadi Cherith (1 Kings 17:2-6), east of the Jordan. A wadi in the Near East is a seasonal riverbed that at times (usually during the rainy season) carries water. When the water of the wadi finally dries up, God tells Elijah to go to the Phoenician town of Zarephath, some 8 miles (13 kilometers) south of Sidon and 14 miles (22 kilometers) north of Tyre.

Zarephath or Sarepta (modern Sarafand) was excavated by archaeologist James Pritchard in 1969. The results of the excavation suggest that the city was a prosperous harbor and commercial center during the time of Elijah in the ninth century B.C. Pritchard unearthed more than 20 pottery kilns, suggesting that the town may have been an important center of pottery production. Located on the coast of the Mediterranean, Zarephath was also known for the production of purple dye, which was extracted from a local shell.[1]

Phoenicia was the name of the coastal strip, located now in modern Lebanon, that was dominated by major city-states such as Sidon, Tyre, and Byblos. The name became more common during the first millennium B.C. Most probably, its inhabitants represented a mix of the original Canaanite population with later immigrants who had come from somewhere in the Mediterranean basin. The names *Phoenicia* and *Phoenicians* may have been derived from a Greek term *phoinos,* which means "red," and was most likely a reference to one of the most typical Phoenician products, i.e., the purple dye made from shells and used in the clothing and weaving industries.[2]

Israel's interaction with Phoenicia was both positive and negative. During the times of David and Solomon Phoenicia became the gross supplier of excellent timber (1 Kings 5:8-10) as well as highly qualified craftsmen who helped in the building of the Temple and other monumental buildings (2 Chron. 2:13, 14). In return for this help Solomon gave Hiram of Tyre 20 towns in Galilee (1 Kings 9:10-14; 2 Chron. 8:2).

Phoenician sailors were world-renowned for their navigational and sailing skills, and the two maritime expeditions mentioned in the Bible included not only Israelite sailors but also Phoenician experts.[3] Unfortunately, Israel did not only use the skilled craftsmen and sailors from Phoenicia, but they also became fascinated with Phoenician religion and deities, which were worshipped from the time of Solomon (1 Kings 11:5) until the reform under King Josiah (2 Kings 23:13). The most negative reference to Phoenicia is connected with the alliance made by the Israelite King Omri with the king of Sidon, Ethbaal (1 Kings 16:31), resulting in the marriage of Omri's son, Ahab, to Ethbaal's daughter, Jezebel (1 Kings 18:18, 19). This marriage introduced an age where the worship of Baal, in contrast to the exclusive worship of Yahweh, became the state-sponsored cult in Israel.

Action

All the action of this story begins with the phrase the "word of the Lord" (1 Kings 17:8). God speaks again to Elijah hiding away at wadi Cherith and gives him a new GPS location. Surprisingly, He wants Elijah out of Israelite territory and sends him to the Phoenician harbor town of Zarephath, advising him that He had already worked on the heart of a widow who would feed him (1 Kings 17:9). Interestingly, the Hebrew text states that God had already "commanded" (NIV, NKJV, NASB) a widow. Did Elijah wonder about God commanding a woman—a foreigner—and especially one from neighboring Phoenicia, whose princess Jezebel was the current queen of Israel and had had such a devastating influence upon the religious orientation of the royal court and the people as a whole?

Elijah obeys, and as he is about to enter the city gates, he sees a widow, most likely marked by a certain type of dress, gathering sticks. He demands water—a common request that was generally fulfilled by everybody, as hospitality was a key value of ancient Semitic societies. His second request for food is also normal, even though much more complicated during a time of drought and famine.

The widow's reply in 1 Kings 17:12 is surprising, as she makes reference to Yahweh, the God of Israel. We wonder if she could tell by Elijah's dress that he was a special man of God or maybe she could tell from his accent that he was from the south or, perhaps, God had somehow prepared the way and had made her receptive to the divine "command" (verse 9).

God's message, delivered via Elijah, to the widow begins with the often repeated "fear not"[4] and concludes with a wonderful promise of unlimited oil and flour supplies. It must have felt like the land of milk and honey—but then, talk is cheap. The woman's faith is visible by the description of her execution of Elijah's request. She just goes and does it (verse 15).

The story could end here—a nice happy ending with many significant theological undertones. However, tragedy is just around the corner. Sometime later, her young boy becomes ill and finally breathes his last.[5]

The reaction of the woman is understandable and echoes the pain she must have felt at that moment. Her husband is dead. And now her son, her only hope of future care, is also dead. Elijah is not offended. He senses her pain and disregards her accusations. He carries the young lad to his rooftop room and lays him upon his own bed. He cries to God, echoing some of the questions that were already expressed by the widow (1 Kings 17:18, 20), and then he positions himself three times upon the dead child—and the miracle happens. God listens and hears Elijah's plea. The child is alive and is returned to his mother's arms. Immediately, she recognizes the omnipotence of Yahweh. He is not just the territorial God of Israel, limited by the borders of the kingdoms of Israel and Judah. He is the Creator and Sustainer of the entire earth, including Phoenicia.

Digging Deep

1 Kings 17 revolves around the conflict between Yahweh (or the Lord, how most English versions represent the Hebrew word marking the God of Israel in the Old Testament)[6] and Baal. As already noted, geography and location are important tools in shaping a story. Several centuries later, Jesus referenced this story and its location: "I assure you that there were many widows in Israel in Elijah's time, when the sky was shut for three and a half years and there was a severe famine throughout the land. Yet Elijah was not sent to any of them, but to a widow in Zarephath in the region of Sidon" (Luke 4:25, 26, NIV). Elijah was not sent to an Israelite widow or somebody living in Judah—God marched him right into the heart of Phoenicia, the center of Baalism. It was here that God would defeat the Canaanite storm god that had captured the imagination of the Israelite court and its people. Thus, Carmel was just the logical follow-up on the outcome of the battle between the Lord and Baal.

The first victory for the Lord is the expression of faith—even though small and fragile—that the widow of Zarephath, being a Phoenician herself and most likely steeped in Baalism, expresses by her willingness to risk her last flour and oil to make some food for the tired prophet (1 Kings 17:15). After her conversation with Elijah she goes and does what was needed. She does not spend time discussing truth and looking at the important metaphysical issues revolving around the question of God's existence and His power to intervene. She is willing to act. Baal 0, Yahweh 1.

Note her response in 1 Kings 17:12 to Elijah's request for food: "As surely as the Lord [= Yahweh] your God lives . . ." (NIV). Somehow, the widow recognized Elijah as belonging to Yahweh. Perhaps it was his dress.

Perhaps it was his behavior. We don't know since the biblical text does not state this explicitly. However, it is still "your God." While there may have been a little seed of faith that responds to Elijah's request, the widow still has a long way to go in her personal faith journey.

The next step in her experience with Yahweh is described in 1 Kings 17:16. Every morning the jar of flour is full, with enough to spare for her household guest. Every morning the jar of oil is full, and day by day she can observe—up close and personal—that the word of the God of Israel can be trusted. He is not like Baal or any other Canaanite god or goddess. Yahweh is different. He keeps His word. Baal 0, Yahweh 2.

As we said before, the story could end here and everyone would be happy. A widow and her family have been saved from starvation. The prophet of God is being taken care of. Things look good.

But life is not like Hollywood wants us to believe it is. Life is painful. Life is not fair. Life on planet earth is the war zone in this cosmic battle between God and Satan, and sin causes pain. The widow's son suddenly falls sick and verse 17 gives us a glimpse of his progression from bad to worse. He just fades away and one day breathes his last. The widow's painful cry to Elijah provides us a picture of her tormented soul. Following along the lines of a long-established train of thought, she thinks that it must be her sin that caused her son's death (verse 18). Her image of deities is determined by the theology that she knows, and one of the pillars of ancient Near Eastern theology (including Baalism) is that deities are generally not benign and can easily be upset if their temple or shrine is not cared for appropriately. The widow feels that Yahweh has now caught up with her sins. Baal 1, Yahweh 2.

But the Lord is not like the other gods. He is not vindictive and does not enjoy the death (or pain) of humanity; He is the exact opposite. He was willing to give of Himself so that everyone who believes in Him will have eternal life (John 3:16). But this was still in the future. Elijah seems to recognize the crucial moment in the theological thinking of the widow of Zarephath, and he cries to the Creator to restore life to this young Phoenician. This is another ground zero moment in the battle between God and Satan. One prayer and one life, affecting the faith of a foreigner. But God is active and not far removed. He hears the prayers of His servant,[7] and the boy is miraculously brought back to life (verse 22). Baal 1, Yahweh 3.

As Elijah hands the boy to his mother, the seedling of faith continues to grow. Her response shows a changed theological perspective. The widow has moved away from the image of a vindictive and even arbitrary god to one who is compassionate and caring and—most importantly—powerful. She now believes that Yahweh lives and is involved in the lives of those who put their trust in Him. Baal 1, Yahweh 4. While the war was not over in the cosmic conflict, one battle had been won. It is good to remember that this battle happened outside the territory of Israel, on Phoenician soil, highlighting the fact that the God of the Old Testament (and reiterated in the New Testament) is a universal God and not just limited to national boundaries (Rom. 3:29).

Issues

Being alone: Widows in the ancient Near East were in a precarious situation. In a male-dominated society they had minimal legal protection. The nameless widow of Zarephath, while not bereft of children, had to fend for her family alone. She could not sit down with her husband in the dusk after a busy day working the fields and share her joys and concerns. She did not only have to keep the house tidy and the food ready, she had to provide some type of income that would put something into her cooking pots.

"Widowhood" seems to have multiplied by a major factor in the twenty-first century. Most "widows" (if we may stretch the term) do not lose their husbands (or their wives) through death. Nowadays, husbands (or wives) walk out on their families, shack up with another partner, or unceremoniously ask for a quick divorce settlement since "it just won't work." So, the modern widows and widowers end up becoming single parents (if children are involved, which, unfortunately, seems to be the case in most circumstances) who have to provide shelter, food, love, discipline, fun, moral values, religion, and a myriad of other things to their disintegrating families. Besides the ever-existing need for more time, they are alone. The extended family usually does not live close by, and even if that were the case, most grandparents, uncles, and aunts are kept so busy by the demands of modern society that they have little energy and strength left to give to single-parent families.

Being alone means that there is nobody to serve as a backup, a counterpart, a much needed discussion partner who can give constructive and (lovingly) critical feedback. Being alone means that you always feel like the fifth wheel when you visit your friends whose families are intact. Being alone means that you receive few hugs and kisses (instead, you're always doling them out).

The good news is that God loves widows and single parents. Together with orphans, strangers, and the poor they seem to be a major concern for the God who created the entire universe (Ex. 22:21-24; Deut. 10:18; 27:19; Ps. 68:5; Jer. 49:11). That's why He sent Elijah to the widow of Zarephath. Jesus shows a special concern for widows. Parallel to our story, Jesus resurrects the only son of a widow living in Nain (Luke 7:11-15) and highlights the faithfulness of a widow who gave freely of the little she had (Mark 12:41-44). In the early church widows represented a focal point for the ministry of the church (Acts 4:34; 6:1-7; James 1:27).

How do you relate to single parents in your circle of friends? How does your church support the increasing number of families who are in desperate need of not only material goods, but even more of love and warmth and care?

Being alone is not always easy. However, God loves and cares for the lonely in a special way.

Re-action

Chantal: Having Elijah around wasn't always easy for the widow of Zarephath. Even today I sometimes find that being around truly godly people isn't always easy. By association with them I begin to see more glaringly my own flaws. Sometimes I am inclined to withdraw and associate myself with people that I "fit in" with better. Perhaps, like the widow, God has some special blessing for me as I am challenged to better live my everyday life in God's presence.

Gerald: Widows seem to be particularly generous. The widow of Zarephath is no exception here. Perhaps it is lack of material things and loneliness that causes us to be more ready to give freely? It seems that living on the edge, without our much desired social safety nets, helps us to cultivate more faith. I remember many moments in our own family history where God came through in the last moment, especially considering the material needs of our family. Lord, help me to remember these moments and protect me from feeling "safety" in checking or saving accounts, a nice and comfortable home, and a regular paycheck!

---

[1] See Ray L. Roth, "Zarephath (Place)," in *Anchor Bible Dictionary*, vol. 6, p. 1041. Compare also Dale W. Manor, "Zarephath," in *The New Interpreter's Dictionary of the Bible*, vol. 5, pp. 956, 957.

[2] Claude Doumet-Serhal, "Phoenicia," in *The New Interpreter's Dictionary of the Bible*, vol. 4, p. 517.

[3] 1 Kings 10:22 mentions an expedition to Tarshish that employed Phoenicians as part of the maritime team. Another reference is made to a trip to Ophir (1 Kings 9:26-28) on the Red Sea, which also employed Phoenicians as seamen.

[4] God's call for service is mostly preceded by a "fear not." Compare the stories of Abram (Gen. 15:1), Hagar (Gen. 21:17), Isaac (Gen. 26:24), Israel as a people (Ex. 14:13), Joshua (Joshua 8:1), and numerous other examples from Scripture. For further examples and discussion compare the comprehensive study of Edgar W. Conrad, *Fear Not Warrior: A Study of 'al tîrā ' Pericopes in the Hebrew Scriptures*, Brown Judaic Studies, vol. 75 (Chico, Calif.: Scholars Press, 1985).

[5] The expression denoting his death is unique. Literally it reads: "until he had no breath left in him." It is God's breath (Gen. 2:7) that gives humanity life. When there is no breath left, a person dies. A similar expression is found in Daniel 10:17 where it is used by Daniel in a hyperbolical way to indicate his fragile state and lack of understanding.

[6] This divine name is known as the *tetragrammaton* among Hebrew Bible scholars. Originally, Jewish scribes did not include vowels in the writing of the Hebrew language (similar to modern Hebrew which also does not include specific vowel signs). However, over time (especially following the exile in Babylon), Jews began to use Aramaic as their day-to-day language, and Hebrew became a "sacred language," reserved for the holy writings and temple and synagogue rituals. In order not to forget the original pronunciation, Jewish scholars (beginning in the fourth century A.D.) began to add a system of signs that indicated vocalization. Because of the holiness of God, the *tetragrammaton*, however, was not vocalized, but the vowels of the noun *God* (Hebrew *'elohim*) were added, thus creating a hybrid word whose exact pronunciation is not known. Looking at the linguistic data would suggest a pronunciation of Yahweh.

[7] This motif reappears in Elijah's taunt of the Baal prophets in 1 Kings 18:27.

Chapter 12

Gehazi:
Missing the Mark

Imagine...

Imagine if the prophet Elisha had been asked to fill out an evaluation form for Gehazi:

SUPERVISOR EVALUATION OF APPRENTICE
Private and Confidential

Apprentice Name: Gehazi
Position: Apprentice to the prophet Elisha
Employer: The God of the universe

Purpose:
This is a confidential report in the process of evaluating an apprentice's progress in the apprenticeship program. An honest and thoughtful evaluation should pinpoint strengths and weaknesses of the candidate and should indicate whether or not the candidate should continue with the apprenticeship.

Instructions:
Carefully read and evaluate each characteristic, trait, or ability.

Work Habits
Appearance and dress for work
Gehazi has always been concerned about outward appearances and goes to great lengths to maintain them.

Grasp of the work situation
Although Gehazi has a very good theoretical knowledge of God and has seen firsthand many examples of His power, he strangely seems to be lacking a personal

109

relationship with God. He shows little interest in God's national or international plans and seems unaware of his role in helping or hindering them.

Follows instructions

Gehazi is highly intelligent and creative, which is one of the reasons that he was selected for this apprenticeship. He is quick to assess a situation and demonstrates the ability to make full use of circumstances. Unfortunately, he does not always explicitly follow instructions.

Attitude:

Acceptance of working conditions

Unfortunately, Gehazi seems to have misunderstood the office of prophet. He does not seem to realize that a great leader must be prepared to serve everyone. Gehazi has never embraced the reality that prophets are often not popular or wealthy. And he seems to assume that the current apprenticeship is a stepping-stone to power and influence.

Courtesy and sensitivity to others

At the beginning of his apprenticeship period Gehazi showed great sensitivity to others and was able to assess situations and needs of individuals well. Regrettably, this sensitivity to others has completely faded out.

Work ethic

Gehazi's work ethic, unfortunately, is exemplified by a recent event in which he obtained a large sum of money and several designer outfits by falsifying information.

Continuation in apprenticeship program

Gehazi has been in this program for many years, and I was hoping that he would be able to fill my position after my retirement. He really did seem to have all the necessary talents and aptitudes. Sadly, Gehazi has let the opportunity afforded him by this program slip by and no longer appears to have the necessary dedication or calling to continue.

Supervisor name (please print and sign)
Elisha

Meet the Cast

Gehazi: As the servant of the prophet, he was generally considered to be the natural successor (see the Elijah-Elisha handover in 2 Kings 2) of the prophet. Gehazi appears three times in the Elisha stories. First, he acts as a go-between in Elisha's interaction with the Shunammite woman (2 Kings 4). He makes his second appearance in the miraculous healing of Naaman, the Syrian army commander (2 Kings 5). Finally, he reappears at the royal Israelite court where he is telling King Joram about the deeds of Elisha (2 Kings 8:1-6). Gehazi's motives are not clear, and his character is dubious.

Elisha: His name means "God saves," and he is predominantly known as a hands-on miracle-worker. This focus on action over reflection or teaching may be due to the historiographical interest of the biblical material. Elisha ministered predominantly in the northern kingdom of Israel, even though he appears to have had dealings with some of the kings of the surrounding nations of Moab, Edom, and Syria. As a prophet (and a precursor to the major classical prophets, such as Isaiah, Amos, or Hosea of the eighth century B.C.), he interacts significantly with the marginalized. He provides a huge supply of oil for a widow (2 Kings 4:1-7), he transforms the bad water of a spring so that a small community has a dependable water resource (2 Kings 2:19-22), and he feeds 100 men with only 20 small barley rolls (2 Kings 4:42-44). His wise counsel to kings bespeaks a careful thinker and listener, someone who is able to listen to God's quiet voice.

Naaman: His Semitic name means "to be pleasant." Naaman was the commander-in-chief of the Aramean army, which had its capital in Damascus, Syria, during the ninth century B.C. He is portrayed as a good soldier, much appreciated by his king and family, who suddenly finds himself struck by a disease—leprosy—which struck terror in the hearts of the ancients. It is not clear if his skin condition is identical to Hansen's disease, the modern name for leprosy, or if it just involved skin rashes. Even though it may not have been Hansen's disease, it may have led to his isolation and quarantine, thus potentially crippling his capacity to work, worship, and interact with other people.

King of Israel: Neither the king of Aram nor the king of Israel are mentioned by name. This is not a story about kings and royal courts (even though they appear) but about a foreigner being healed by the God of Israel. It avoids chronological concerns in order to tell a story of faith and greed in a more abstract way.

Background Information

Naaman and Elisha lived during the ninth century B.C. in a time marked by increasing international fragmentation of power. Elisha's ministry was focused upon the northern kingdom of Israel. The divided kingdoms of Israel and Judah developed differently during those years. In northern Israel, the house of Omri was the first dynasty to successfully develop some type of succession (Omri, Ahab, Ahaziah, Jehoram). They also established a new capital at Samaria. Both biblical as well as extrabiblical sources document the increasing rivalry and military tension between the northern kingdom of Israel and the Aramean states to its north (1 Kings 20, 22; 2 Kings 6:8-7:20), which is only occasionally reversed in moments when stronger external enemies threaten the region.[1]

This underlying tension between Aram and Israel also explains the strong reaction of the nameless Israelite king when he receives the diplomatic letter of introduction from the (also nameless) Aramean king for his general Naaman, requesting that Naaman be cured (2 Kings 5:6, 7).

It is also during this time that the surrounding "nations" (such as the Ammonites, Moabites, or Edomites) begin to rebel against the yoke of Israelite domination (2 Kings 3). Ahab's second son, Jehoram, is reported to have led an unsuccessful Israelite expedition against the Moabites via the desert of Edom (2 Kings 3:4-27), which may be in retaliation for a rebellion that may also have been described in the famous Mesha stele.[2]

Judah's history during the ninth century B.C. involves three kings: Jehoshaphat, Jehoram of Judah (same name as one of the sons of Ahab), and Ahaziah of Judah. Of these three, Jehoshaphat is the most important leader of Judah, making peace with Israel (1 Kings 22:44) and, unfortunately, even establishing an alliance with the house of Ahab. Second Kings 8:18-26 describes how Jehoshaphat's son, Jehoram, married Ahab's daughter, Athaliah, who assumes the throne herself after the death of her son, Ahaziah, and proceeds to kill off the entire royal family (or at least she thought that she had gotten them all!) in order to secure her own rule (2 Kings 11:1). This alliance between Israel and Judah, between the idolatrous, albeit powerful, house of Omri and the house of Jehoshaphat, unfortunately pulled down the Judean kings.

Action

Naaman's story begins with the capture of a young Israelite girl by marauding Aramean troops who ends up in the household of an important royal courtier of the king of Aram, located in Damascus (2 Kings 5:2). When Naaman and his family realize the gravity of his skin disease,[3] it is the nameless servant girl who advises her mistress of a famous prophet, living in Samaria, who can cure her master of leprosy. A chain of events is set into motion by this short remark that guides the development of the story. Naaman advises his boss, the king of Aram, who in turn agrees to send a rather demanding letter to the king of Israel (2 Kings 5:5, 7). Faced with the humanly impossible request, the Israelite king is desperate and ready to prepare for the inevitable war. However, Elisha, having heard of his plight, sends him a message and suggests that Naaman be sent to him.

When Naaman arrives at the doorstep of the prophet, no special courtesies are offered to him. No red carpet. No private interview with the miracle worker. No special attention by the prophet's staff. All he receives is a sentence from Gehazi, the prophet's servant, indicating that in order to be healed he should dip seven times in the Jordan River. Gehazi must have been pleased. Finally, Elisha was entering the international market and would soon be a globally recognized brand name. Obviously, as the servant of Elisha,[4] he would be riding the wave of success with him.

Naaman is not delighted with this prescription. As a proud Aramean, he points to the much bigger rivers up north, but at the insistence of his servants, he takes the leap of faith. He follows the instructions and dips seven times in the river. After the sixth time, nothing has happened. But after the seventh time, the miracle can be seen. His skin is as good as new, and joyously he returns to Elisha to present him with the customary gifts. Miracle workers must be paid in order to assure future beneficial treatment. Elisha refuses to receive any payment. Rather, he takes this opportune moment to share with Naaman about his relationship to the only God, Yahweh, who has healed him. Following Naaman's happy departure, Gehazi slips out of the house and, taking a shortcut, catches up with the Syrian party.

He fabricates a story and—to his delight—receives two talents (roughly 150 pounds, or 68 kg) of silver and two sets of clothes. Life is good. He will never have to worry about food for tomorrow. He will *be* somebody because he *has* something. As he returns to Elisha's home, he seeks to cover his tracks.

But Elisha is waiting for him with one question: "Where have you been, Gehazi?" (2 Kings 5:25). As Gehazi continues to spin his distorted view of reality (we may also safely call this a "lie"), Elisha confronts him with reality. How could he have hoped that his master would not be aware of this—he who raised the dead, fed the hungry and poor, and knows what a Gentile king whispers in his bedroom (2 Kings 6:12)? Even if he thought he could trick Elisha, how could he have hoped to sidestep the Lord, the One in whose name Elisha performed all these miraculous acts?

Using another rhetorical question, Elisha drives home his point: this is not the time to accumulate things, but rather to focus on serving the Creator of the universe, the One who can raise the dead and heal the leper. Judgment comes quickly in Gehazi's case, and he is struck with Naaman's skin disorder—being at the same time a rich member of society. It is unlikely that he continued his ministry with Elisha. He reappears once more in 2 Kings 8:4 where he is conversing with the king of Israel about his past master.

Digging Deep

For our *Digging Deep* section we will focus on the brief conversation that the prophet Elisha had with Gehazi in 2 Kings 5:25. To begin, let's look back on the relationship that Elisha had had with his predecessor, the great prophet Elijah. Elisha prepared for his prophetic ministry by the practical daily experience of serving the prophet Elijah (1 Kings 19:21). Although the two were very close, Elisha understood who he was really serving. He understood that Elijah was performing his miracles by the power of God's Spirit. When Elijah was taken from earth by an impressive heavenly transport system, Elisha knew exactly what he needed to do to carry on the work—a double share of the Spirit that Elijah had (2 Kings 2:9). In learning to serve Elijah well, Elisha had also learned to teach and lead well. Although we are not given any details about his calling, we know that by Gehazi being chosen as the servant of Elisha, he in turn was being offered the same opportunities that Elisha had been given.

This brings us to the exchange between Elisha and Gehazi in 2 Kings 5. Gehazi has just run after Naaman and through deception made a quick fortune. Now, he comes back to Elisha's house and seems to think that he can go on with his duties as if nothing has happened. After all the years of working with Elisha, he really should know that God cannot be fooled. This is probably why God deals so severely with deceit in all its forms. Lies are an extremely effective way of keeping us from God. This is why God hates lies so much (Prov. 12:22), and let's not forget that Satan is described as the father of all lies (John 8:44). Lies have two purposes, which usually go together and can be seen easily in the case of Gehazi. Lies are used to trick people into giving us what we are not honestly entitled to as Gehazi did with Namaan. Lies can also be used to try to cover our shame and avoid exposure to others. This avoidance of exposure and consequences is what motivated Gehazi's lie when asked where he had been (2 Kings 5:26). Both of these purposes work against what God has in mind for His children. As we live by the golden rule, we will be eager to give as much of ourselves to others as possible. The Godhead figured out a way to give to fallen humanity even before they fell. This shows the very fundamental difference between God and Satan. God is all about giving of Himself. Satan is all about taking for himself what does not belong to him.

Jesus never had to lie to cover up something He had done; instead, He modeled a very different way of handling things that made Him afraid. Rather than trying to lie His way out of a situation, Jesus prayed and asked God to take Him out of situations that were threatening and then—if God did not provide a way out of these situations—Jesus drew on God's strength to face the situation (Matt. 26:39).

Imagine a little girl with chocolate smears around her mouth looking at you with the most innocent eyes she can muster and telling you that she has absolutely no idea as to who has been sampling the cake. As long as she holds to her lie, your relationship is affected. As soon as she admits her guilt, the consequences can be taken care of and the relationship can be repaired. We all stand before God with a lot more than chocolate smears around our mouths: "Nothing in all creation is hidden from God's sight. Everything is uncovered and laid bare before the eyes of him to whom we must give account" (Heb. 4:13, NIV). As long as we keep trying to pretend that we do not need God's help, He cannot help us.

Gehazi had so many opportunities over the years to experience firsthand God's power and to know that God really can see us. After running after Namaan, Gehazi did not hand in his resignation to Elisha and said that he would rather go into business. Instead of being upfront with Elisha and saying that he had chosen not to serve God, Gehazi simply kept lying and pretending while in God's service. Gehazi's attitude, an attitude of lying and stealing, must have built up over the years and reached its culmination at this moment.

Issues

Familiarity with the holy: People who live in the presence of an important person tend to often forget the importance of that person. After all, they see the faults and blemishes of that person on a daily basis. I imagine that the employees of the queen of England do not always stand in awe of Her Majesty but begin to see their work as just another job. People that walk, talk, and live in the presence of the Holy (such as ministers, professors of religion, Bible teachers, or church administrators) face the danger of becoming familiar with the Holy.

The Gehazi syndrome of becoming familiar with the Holy is not limited to the servant of Elisha living in the ninth century B.C. It is something that can affect us—even if we are not religious "professionals" getting paid by the church or another nonprofit entity. As we pray, read Scripture, and talk about God, we can be in danger of forgetting who this God really is. We may become preoccupied with our material situation. We may worry about our apparel and dress. We may recite our morning and evening prayers as part of a well-known routine, but forget the core of worship, i.e., the commitment and love reserved for a loving, personal Creator and Savior who is eager to spend quality time with us.

Here are three possible strategies that may help us overcome this common "disease" and renew our commitment to God:

1. Remember your first love for Jesus. Recall and recount how He came into your life and what made you decide to follow Him.

2. Block out time for personal prayer, and make this time count. Keep a prayer journal, and keep reading in it. When we talk and listen to the Creator of the universe and our personal Savior, our mouths must drop open in awe and wonder. He truly cares—even about wayward, tired servants who may have momentarily lost their way.

3. Find a prayer partner to whom you can be accountable. This should be a person whom you trust and who loves the Lord. Be open about your struggles. This is the moment where you can let down your guard and feel safe about doing so.

Gehazi obviously blew it and paid a high price for this greed. However, his story is not only part of a historical review of Israel's past—both glorious and glum—but it is included for our benefit so that we can learn from it and avoid the pitfall that trapped Gehazi into seeking riches and losing his intimacy with God. After all, "all Scripture is God-breathed and is useful for teaching, rebuking, correcting, and training in righteousness" (2 Tim. 3:16, NIV).

Re-action

Chantal: Gehazi's story reminds me of the truth that hanging out in a garage doesn't make me a car. Gehazi had so many opportunities to see God working powerfully, and yet he seems so totally oblivious to the big picture—all he can see is coats and money. Gehazi has totally lost the ability to see the world through God's eyes. I'm left wondering what could have been. Sadly, we will never know what Gehazi could have been as God's man. I don't want to look back on my life and wonder what potential I could have had. I want to let God transform me and enable me to live life to the fullest without regrets.

Gerald: As a pastor, longtime professor of theology, and missionary, I have seen a number of colleagues and friends fall beside the way. I know that I am not better, so what made them stumble and what keeps me toddling along? It cannot be anything inside me. Rather, it is the constant reminder that my wise mother keeps putting before me at opportune moments: "Gerald, stay humble and stick close to God." I guess that's the secret. Sticking close to God, allowing the Holy Spirit to do some major remodeling, and remembering that the new model is not in any way due to my great efforts but just "amazing grace."

---

[1] The Neo-Assyrian King Shalmaneser III lists Ahab of Israel among a coalition of Syrian and Palestinian kings who fought the Assyrian army at Qarqar, on the river Orontes, north of Hamath in southern Syrian in the sixth year of his reign, namely 853 B.C. Cf. Gershon Galil, "Shalmaneser III in the West," *Revue Biblique* 109.1 (2002), pp. 40-56, and Provan, Long, and Longman, *A Biblical History of Israel* pp. 264, 265. For the text of the inscription mentioning Ahab, see K. Lawson Younger, Jr., "Neo-Assyrian Inscriptions: Shalmaneser III (2.113)," in *The Context of Scripture: Volume 2: Monumental Inscriptions from the Biblical World,* ed. William W. Hallo and K. Lawson Younger, Jr. (Leiden, Netherlands: Brill, 2000), pp. 261-264.

[2] The adventurous story of the discovery of the Mesha stele can be found in M. Patrick Graham, "The Discovery and Reconstruction of the Mesha Inscription," in *Studies in the Mesha Inscription and Moab*, ed. J. Andrew Dearman, Archaeology and Biblical Studies, vol. 2 (Atlanta, Ga.: Scholars Press, 1989), pp. 41-92. For a good reconstruction of the historical context, see J. Andrew Dearman, "Historical Reconstruction and the Mesha Inscription," in *Studies in the Mesha Inscription and Moab*, pp. 155-210.

[3] The biblical text in 2 Kings 5:1 uses the Hebrew term denoting leprosy, a skin disease requiring quarantine and connoting impurity (cf. Lev. 13:44, 45). As already noted, it is not clear if the modern definition of Hansen's disease (i.e., leprosy) is identical to the use of the Hebrew term.

[4] Note that the Hebrew term describing the quality of the "servanthood" of Elisha (1 Kings 19:21) is the same that describes the relationship between Moses and Joshua (Joshua 1:1) and is not the typical word used to describe regular servants.

Chapter 13

Baruch: Building a Legacy in a Crumbling World

Imagine...

Imagine reading the following book review:

Jeremiah son of Hilkiah, as dictated to Baruch son of Neriah, *The Words of Jeremiah*, Temple Library Series, vol. 15 (Jerusalem: Library of the Temple Publishers, 580 B.C.), 52 chapters. Only available in one parchment copy and therefore priceless. Selections have been reproduced, and limited editions have been reported in Babylon.

This book is a collection of numerous prophetic visions directed at both individuals and the Jewish nation as a whole. While this compilation was transcribed by Baruch, Jeremiah closely supervised the work. Although intricately involved in the production and distribution of the work, Baruch denies any involvement in influencing or editing the contents (Jer. 36:18). The current volume is an amplification of the first shorter volume, which was deliberately destroyed by King Jehoiakim (36:32). The book consists of various visions and sermons set in the historical time frame of the last days of the kingdom of Judah. The fact that this is much more pertinent and personal than a scholarly historical review is underlined by the insightful biographical data given throughout the volume. Both author and transcriber faced violent opposition during the writing process. The author encouraged submission to Babylon and warned against trying to form an alliance with Egypt. The book uses the proverbial "stick and carrot" method with prophecies—it presents the dismal results of disobedience balanced with the glorious descriptions of a future for those who love God, in which they will be united under a "righteous Branch . . . from David's line" (Jer. 33:15). This book is a must-read, not only for those in leadership positions but for anyone who is serious about finding personal direction in times of political and economic chaos. The literary quality as well as the viability of the many predictions is bound to stand the test of time.

Meet the Cast

Baruch: His name means "blessed," and he surely was a blessing to the prophet Jeremiah. He appears four times in the book of Jeremiah (32:12-16; 36; 43:1-7; 45), and since his father's name, Neriah, is mentioned in most of these references, he appears to have been a member of a well-respected Judean family. Jeremiah 51:59 describes Seraiah, the quartermaster (NKJV) of the last king of Judah, Zedekiah, as a son of Neriah and thus, possibly, a brother of Baruch. As a scribe, Baruch was a member of an elite group of people who certified land transactions, wrote down significant administrative texts and decrees, and participated in the governance of a country.

Jeremiah: Prophet of Yahweh, Jeremiah is originally from Anathoth in the territory of Benjamin, some 3 miles (4.5 kilometers) northeast of Jerusalem, and a member of a priestly family. Jeremiah was called to a prophetic ministry in 627 B.C., the thirteenth year of king Josiah (Jer. 1:2), and he ministered in Jerusalem as God's mouthpiece until the final destruction of the city in 586 B.C. by the Babylonians. Most likely due to Daniel's intervention at the court of Nebuchadnezzar and his clear pro-Babylonian messages, the Babylonian king took pains to locate the persecuted prophet and free him after the fall of Jerusalem (Jer. 39:11-14; 40:1-6). Following the final revolt by renegade Judean leadership against the Babylonian-appointed governor, Gedaliah, Jeremiah is taken against his will to Egypt where he continues to serve as God's prophet and most likely dies (Jer. 41; 43).

Josiah: Josiah is the last good king of Judah, who takes the throne after the short reign of his godless father, Amon (2 Kings 21:19-26), and begins an amazing reformation and political renaissance in Judah (c. 640-609 B.C.). He comes to the throne at the age of 8 and prematurely dies in the battle of Megiddo against the Egyptian Pharaoh Necho (2 Kings 23:29, 30). Second Chronicles 34:3 tells us that by the age of 16 (after reigning for eight years) Josiah begins to seek the God of his father David, and four years later he starts to actively purge Judah and Jerusalem from its idolatrous practices. When Josiah turns 26, he begins to repair the Jerusalem Temple (2 Kings 22:3-5), and during the restoration process, workmen find the book of the law,[1] which leads to further reforms in Judah.

Jehoiakim: As the second son of Josiah (2 Kings 23:36; 1 Chron. 3:15; 2 Chron. 36:5), he becomes king of Judah in 609 B.C., following the brief reign of his firstborn brother, Jehoahaz, who was exiled to Egypt by Pharaoh Necho (2 Kings 23:31-35). His reign is marked by an increasing downward trend, both spiritually and politically. Having heard the "first edition" of Jeremiah's prophecies read to him, he decides to use the scroll of the "Word of the Lord" as useful kindling material for his winter stove (Jer. 36:23). Jehoiakim dies just prior to the second Babylonian invasion of Jerusalem in 598 B.C.

Zedekiah: He is Judah's last king, who had been installed by Nebuchadnezzar after the fall of Jerusalem in 597 B.C. Zedekiah's birth name was Mattaniah, and he was a younger son of Josiah. His new name can be translated as "the Lord is my righteousness," but instead of living up to this name, Zedekiah's vacillating actions put Jerusalem on the course of definite destruction. Jeremiah's numerous interventions with Zedekiah are to no avail (Jer. 21; 34; 37; 38:14-28), and Jerusalem and the Temple are finally destroyed in 586 B.C after a three-year siege by the Babylonian troops. The last king of Judah is taken prisoner as he tries to escape from the burning city. After witnessing the execution of his sons, he is blinded and sent in chains to Babylon (Jer. 39:4-7).

Background Information

Baruch lived in a time of tremendous political and spiritual upheaval. Josiah's reign marks Judah's last chance to avoid destruction and judgment, but unfortunately, the last righteous king of Judah dies a premature death. After the death of the last important Neo-Assyrian king, Ashurbanipal, in 633 B.C., a number of mediocre Assyrian rulers lead to unrest and loss of central control, facilitating more power to the vassal states, including Judah. It was during this time that Babylon's ruler, Nabopolassar, father of Nebuchadnezzar, establishes the rising star of the Neo-Babylonian empire in 626 B.C. and together with the Medes begins to attack the Assyrian strongholds of Nineveh (612 B.C.), Haran (610/609 B.C.), and Carchemish (605 B.C.). The biblical narrative of these events has been enriched and confirmed by the discovery of the Babylonian Chronicles, containing a formal description of the Babylonian affairs of state (albeit incomplete), beginning in 745 B.C. and reaching into 538 B.C.[2]

Scribes in the time of Baruch (and also earlier) represented a powerful class of administrative leaders whose qualifications went beyond the mere recording of events or numbers and figures. An ancient scribe should not be confused with a hard-working secretary or even a capable administrative assistant. Scribes in Egypt and Mesopotamia were key members of administrative units and were required to keep an increasingly complex state running smoothly. They were also key for the transmission of wisdom literature, and even though the Old Testament does not contain explicit statements regarding the existence of scribal schools, it is most likely that they existed during the monarchic period. In view of these facts it is important to remember that Baruch's work for Jeremiah was not unimportant or merely clerical but represented a commitment to the unfashionable "word of the Lord" on the part of Baruch, who could have made a better career in the court (as, apparently, his brother did [cf. Jer. 51:59]).

During the 1970s a bulla containing the stamp and name of Baruch appeared on the antiquities market and was subsequently published by Israeli archaeologist Nahman Avigad.[3] While we do not know the exact location where the bulla was found, it is believed to have come from a legal excavation of a section of Jerusalem. Today it is housed in the Israel Museum. Its inscription reads as follows: "Belonging to Berekyahu, son of Neriyahu, the scribe."

Both Berekyahu and Neriyahu are longer forms of the names Baruch and Neriah, attaching the short form of the divine name Yahweh to the biblical name. The fact that Baruch owned his own seal highlights his importance in Judean society.

Many traditions about Baruch have survived in Jewish and Christian sources, portraying him as a wise sage, seer, and Jeremiah's prophetic successor. A number of pseudepigraphic books carrying the name of Baruch exist in Jewish and Christian literature. However, none of these books or their accompanying traditions have a biblical basis.

Action

Jeremiah's ministry (and thus by proxy, Baruch's service) is marked by frequent ups and downs—even though it seems that the downs are predominant. Called as a young man to speak for the Lord (Jer. 1:6), Jeremiah and his friend Baruch witness not only international trouble and upheaval but, even worse, national disaster, personal defamation, and spiritual decline. Following the initial hopeful signs of reform and change under Josiah, the subsequent kings of Judah are either not interested in returning to the God of David or they are so concerned about appearances that they do not amount to anything.

Following Baruch's first writing of Jeremiah's prophecies in the fourth year of King Jehoiakim, c. 605 B.C. (Jer. 36:1), the prophet asks his friend Baruch to stand in his place and read the message on a day of fasting in the Temple (verse 6). It is possible that the day of fasting was called due to the approaching Babylonian danger from the north, which, after the final defeat of the Egyptian-Assyrian coalition at Carchemish in 605 B.C., moved south in order to subjugate the small states of Syria-Palestine. As is always the case in prophetic ministry, the oracles of judgment were intended to move the hardened heart of a people that had, both in practice and theory, left the Lord (verse 7).

Baruch does as requested. After the message is read to the people, the king's advisors request a personal reading of Jeremiah's message (verses 14, 15), and they find the content so disturbing that they recommend reading it to the king. The officials, knowing the moods and loyalties of their king, advise both Jeremiah and Baruch to keep a low profile and carefully present Jeremiah's words to King Jehoiakim. However, if contrition and mourning by the king is hoped for, it does not become a reality. Instead, the king cuts up the scroll, column by column, and burns it in the standing brazier that warms the chamber (verses 23, 24). Nobody is afraid. Nothing is going to change—except, of course, that the king seeks to apprehend and deal with the troublemakers (i.e., Jeremiah and Baruch). Consequently, Baruch goes into hiding.

We do not know what became of Baruch. Did he die in the fall of Jerusalem? Was he taken with Jeremiah to Egypt? The Jewish historian Josephus recorded that when Nebuchadnezzar invaded Egypt, Baruch was taken to Babylon (*Antiquities of the Jews*, 10.179-182), even though we have no historical facts to support this suggestion.

However, Baruch's story does not end with a question mark. Jeremiah records a special message from God as he faces persecution by King Jehoiakim (Jer. 45:1-5). We will return to it in the *Digging Deep* section.

Digging Deep

Have you ever imagined what God would say to you if He sent you a personalized message? I'm not talking about the profound "for God so loved the world that he gave his one and only son" (John 3:16, NIV) or the majestic "and we know that in all things God works for the good of those who love him, who have been called according to his purpose" (Rom 8:28, NIV). No, something personal, especially written for you individually. Few people have had this privilege, but Baruch is one of them. In this section we will take a closer look at Jeremiah 45:1-5 and dig deeper into God's special message to Baruch. We may just discover that He has something special to say to us as well.

The first verse of chapter 45 functions as a type of heading, locating the following verses in time and space. There is a clear link to Jeremiah 36 and the burning of the first scroll. Verse 2 contains a typical messenger formula, indicating the origin of the message, the messenger, and the addressee.

Jeremiah 45:3 does not represent an auspicious opening. God sends a message via Jeremiah, echoing Baruch's lack of hope. We like the translation of the NET Bible, which says, "You have said, 'I feel so hopeless! For the Lord has added sorrow to my suffering. I am worn out from groaning. I can't find any rest.'" Similar to Jeremiah's own moment of despair (Jer. 15:18; 20:7-18), Baruch feels hopeless. By focusing upon his own situation, he seems to have closed all possible avenues of taking courage and finding help.

"The Lord has added sorrow to my suffering" underlines the important Old Testament principle of understanding God as the master of everything—even the bad things that happen to us. The term "sorrow" occurs frequently in the Psalms, especially in psalms of lamentation (cf. Jer. 20:18): sorrow about the terrible word of judgment against Judah and its king; sorrow about missed chances and opportunities.

God's message initially appears to cause even more pain. Is there no hope for God's people and Baruch? The choice of verbs (built—overthrowing, planted—uprooting) echo the call of Jeremiah (Jer. 1:10) and many other references in the book (Jer. 12:14-17; 18:7-9, etc.), representing a major theme in the book of Jeremiah. Somehow one can hear God's own pain in these words. He who wanted to build the perfect city and plant the perfect vineyard (Isa. 7:1-7) has to overthrow and uproot. Judgment is inevitable. Judgment is needed in order to avoid the unchecked viral growth of evil, social injustice, and idolatry.

In Jeremiah 45:5 God asks a rhetorical question and quickly answers it Himself. In essence, He is saying, "Baruch, focus on the larger picture. Do not seek great things for yourself while I am going to bring disaster on *all flesh*" (the same phrase is used in Gen. 6:12, 13). However, there is a divine "but" that allows for hope: "Wherever you go I will let you escape with your life" (NIV).

It is back-to-basics time in Jerusalem and Judah. It is back-to-basics time in Baruch's life. God, the sovereign Creator of the universe, is in control over all human affairs, including Baruch's life. It seems as if God's "you will live" is the counterbalance of the communal downward path. God is still willing to put a stake in human lives, to invest in the unworthy—John 3:16 is still to become a reality.

There is another individual who receives the personal assurance of salvation in the book of Jeremiah, i.e., Ebed-Melech, the servant of Zedekiah from Cush who saved the life of the prophet when he had been thrown into the dry cistern. In Jeremiah 39:18 he also hears this personal assurance.

Issues

How then shall we live? Baruch lived in a time that is a preview of end-times. The world in which he had grown up was about to turn upside down and inside out. On a national scale the kingdom of Judah would find itself as a pawn in the power struggle between Egypt and Babylon for world supremacy. As much as they would have liked to think of themselves as independent, in reality they were not and were repeatedly compelled to take sides.

For us who are living at the close of the world's history there are many similarities between Baruch's world and ours. We are all collectively and individually caught up in the cosmic great controversy between God and Satan. In the end there will be no neutral ground. Through the prophecies of Jeremiah, so faithfully copied and distributed by Baruch, God clearly told them which side to choose. For nearly 50 years God sent detailed messages, foretelling what the consequences would be for their choice of allegiance. We have much more than 50 years of prophecy to look back on. Through the Bible God has given us a very clear prophetic picture of what our future will hold depending on whether we choose God or Satan.

So what was end-time living like for Baruch? Life for Baruch seemed to go on as normal until just before the king of Babylon marched up to the city of Jerusalem. People were striving to get ahead in life. Baruch, with his well-connected family and good education, may have dreamed of a distinguished political career, including a beautiful home and a high standard of living. In our materialistic world most of us feel the pressure to be more and have more. Life seems to be measured by what we have and do rather than what we are. Baruch's end-time should bring our end-time into perspective. When the army of the king of Babylon finally came and put Jerusalem under siege, all that people had been living for suddenly became inconsequential. Of what consequence was a good career in court as Jerusalem suffered an 18-month famine? The great walls would be broken down. Soon their city would be a pile of rubble. The beautifully furnished homes that were the envy of the neighborhood would be nothing but ransacked burnt shells. The Temple that the people regarded as their security would be destroyed. The important positions that everyone desperately wanted would soon be the most dangerous.

Baruch had to live by faith in the prophecies of what was to come even when the wicked were living around him in apparent prosperity (Jer. 12:1-4). People did not like hearing the messages against sin that he was distributing. Calling people to repentance was not popular. Jeremiah ended up in prison (Jer. 38), and Baruch was forced into hiding. The special prophecy given to Baruch at a time when he was discouraged helped him to face his end-time (Jer. 45:1-5). Baruch had learned to see his everyday life in the light of end-time events, and rather than seeking great things for himself, he found and fulfilled his own small duty in supporting the larger purposes of God.

Re-action

Chantal: Nothing seems as solid or unchangeable as the ground we stand on until we experience an earthquake. I remember the surreal sight of the bathroom floor flowing toward me during a powerful quake in Peru. Things that were supposed to be solid suddenly became fluid. Baruch's story has made end-time living once again more vivid for me. Things are not going to grind on as normal forever. Jesus will come again!

Gerald: Being a scribe and a member of an elite group usually guaranteed privileges and open doors. But Baruch seems to surrender these privileges because he believes in Jeremiah's cause and is, himself, listening to Israel's God and is willing to follow Him. I hope that I can see through the trappings of success, education, traditions, and society and focus on the real anchor in life, the one who forsook His privileged position in heaven's court and became a human baby, born into a poor family in Palestine. Baruch, you have been an inspiration to me!

---

[1] It is not entirely clear what this "book of the law" included. It is possible that during the horrific early reign of Josiah's grandfather, Manasseh, the biblical scrolls were burned or destroyed. The discovery of a copy of the law (i.e., possibly the Pentateuch or a section of the Pentateuch) would undoubtedly result in major changes.

[2] A helpful discussion of the historiographical importance of the Babylonian Chronicles can be found in J. A. Brinkman, "The Babylonian Chronicle Revisited," in *Lingering Over Words: Studies in Ancient Near Eastern Literature in Honor of William L. Moran,* ed. T. Abusch et al.; Harvard Semitic Studies, vol. 37 (Atlanta, Ga.: Scholars Press, 1990), pp. 73-104. Compare also Jens Bruun Kofoed, "Fact and Fiction in the Ancient Near East: The Assyrian Royal Inscriptions, the Babylonian Chronicles, and the Books of Kings in the Hebrew Bible," *SEE-J Hiphil* 1 (2004), pp. 1-15, available online at www.see-j.net/index.php/hiphil/issue/view/1 (accessed November 4, 2009).

[3] See Nahman Avigad and Benjamin Sass, *Corpus of West Semitic Stamp Seals* (Jerusalem: Israel Academy of Sciences and Humanities/Israel Exploration Society/Institute of Archaeology, Hebrew University Jerusalem, 1997), pp. 175-176, bulla No. 417.

Epilogue:
The Stories Go On

We have come to the end of retelling the stories of some of the shadow figures of the Old Testament. Their lives have inspired us, have caused us to rethink some of our own convictions and presuppositions, and—last, but not least—have been fun to study.

At times we felt like surgeons, trying to extract a minute blood vessel or nerve ending without overdoing the interpretive task and staying faithful to the confines and intricacies of the Hebrew text. If you knew us personally (and some of you just may!), you would realize how much this experiment in coauthoring, first the *Adult Sabbath School Bible Study Guide* and then the companion volume to this study guide, has changed us as a couple. Coming from different cultural and language backgrounds, we also represent two different ways of writing.

Chantal is the creative member of this team who can see and note things intuitively. Gerald is much more systematic and factual and, being used to academic contexts, prefers to move from A to B in an orderly and systematic manner—and, yes, footnotes documenting a certain proposition should also be included.

Writing about some of the shadow figures of the Old Testament has changed us, and we hope that reading this book and thinking about these individuals has changed you also. Looking at the wonderful (and sometimes surprising) tapestry of Scripture is always exciting. But recognizing that these stories may as well be our stories is even more thrilling.

We hope and pray that the stories continue—we would love to hear your stories. God is still at work in His church and in this world, and by His grace He is using shadow figures to transform people and realities in small or big ways.

One thing we would like to leave with you, our esteemed reader, involves God's amazing Word. We once again realized that Scripture is a never ending pool of new insights, ideas, and concepts that keep surprising us. They are all out there—ready to be discovered and rediscovered and shared.

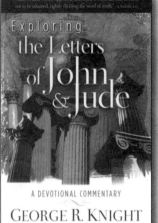
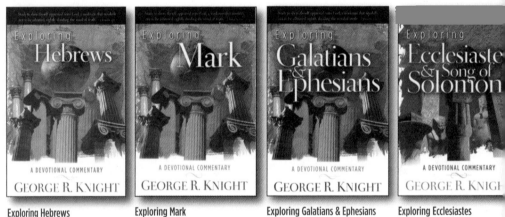